RAINING CATS AND DONKEYS

Feline Frolics
Book Four

Doreen Tovey

SAPERE
BOOKS

RAINING CATS AND DONKEYS

Published by Sapere Books.

11 Bank Chambers, Hornsey, London, N8 7NN,
United Kingdom

saperebooks.com

ISBN: 978-1-912786-15-2

One: Donkeys Get You Like That

Charles said the people who wrote this bilge in the newspapers about donkeys being status symbols were nuts.

At that moment we were in our donkey's paddock dealing with the fact that she'd eaten too many apples, and I couldn't have agreed with him more.

Take the paddock itself, for instance. Ours wasn't the lush green plot surrounded by a neat hedge or smart wire fence such as various of our neighbours kept ponies in. It was a rectangle so bare it looked as if we'd been visited by locusts. Criss-crossed with still barer paths leading to the various lookouts from which Annabel spied on passers-by. Surrounded on three sides by hedges which gave the impression of having had a pudding-basin haircut (eaten, as they were, up to Annabel height in a solid, unvarying line all round the field). And on the fourth side, which separated the paddock from the cottage garden, it sported a wire fence.

The sort of fence one associates with gipsy encampments.

The wire sagging where Annabel leaned on it sling-fashion, or rubbed her stomach in dreamy contemplation when she itched. Other pieces of wire reinforcing the original strands in the places where she had been discovered, at various times, trying to crawl under it on hands and knees. A hurdle gate leaning outwards at a decrepitly drunken angle because Annabel, when she felt like it, used the inside of the gate for resting her bottom on. And just at that moment, in the paddock itself, Annabel with stomach-ache.

She'd been lent to a neighbour to graze down his orchard.

Why people borrowed her when she had a record long enough to send her to Botany Bay was anybody's guess, but there it was. People were always saying could they have her round to be company to their pony for a few days, or they had their grandchildren coming and could Annabel come up on their lawn for the afternoon, or there was a nice bit of grass behind their vegetable plot and it would save them scything it if Annabel could eat it.

The sensible thing, knowing Annabel, would have been to say No to all of them. But how could we when, on the few occasions we had hardened our hearts, the enquirers looked at us as if we were discriminating against them at a prize-giving? So we would say 'Well, if you think you can manage her...' And off would go Annabel, looking like a picture on a birthday card with her Beatle fringe, her shaggy buff coat and her little round white stomach. (Annabel is a Scandinavian-type donkey, which is why, for three parts of the year, she has a yak-like coat and is continually being mistaken for a Shetland pony or an out-size sheepdog). And we would settle down to some gardening with the feeling of parents who have, against their better judgement, allowed a small boy to go to a party and are now pretty certain that he has taken his pea-shooter with him.

They'd be back sooner or later with the inevitability of a boomerang. Annabel had chased the pony. Annabel had eaten the children's ice cream. Annabel — in the case of the grass behind the vegetable plot — had wandered on her tether rope round a rabbit hutch, pulled it over, and dragged it with her like a chain-harrow as she proceeded on her way. For once she herself hadn't eaten anything she shouldn't, but the dragging had opened the hutch door and the rabbits had had a field day in the lettuce.

Annabel in the case of the orchard grass had, on first reporting, behaved herself very well. 'Just reached an apple down here and there,' said the owner of the orchard fondly. 'Nobody'd begrudge the little creature that.'

Whereupon off he pottered towards his Saturday supper, giving the little creature a pat on the rump in parting, and half an hour later we found her rolling on her back in the paddock, her coat damp with sweat, and groaning.

We didn't think it was colic at first. Not just on a couple of apples. Fearing the worst, which had become a habit with us after several years of keeping Siamese cats and two years of keeping a donkey, our thoughts flew to plastic bags. One of these, eaten by an animal, is invariably fatal. We'd been reading about it in our pony book only a few days previously. It blocks the intestines completely and, as there is no indication as to where it lies, nothing can be done about it.

We voiced our fears to our neighbour, Father Adams, who happened by just then as he usually does in moments of crisis. ''Ouldn't surprise I at all', was his reply. 'Old Fred's orchard right by the bus-stop and they there hikers stuffin' theirselves while they wait as if they'm about to cross the Sahara (Father Adams had recently been to see Lawrence of Arabia and references to it coloured his every utterance at the moment) — 'tis a wonder t'aint happened afore'. With which words of comfort — on later reflection we were sure he hadn't thought any such thing, otherwise he'd have stayed and helped us to the last — he, too, proceeded on his way to supper, and I ran for the telephone.

The Vet came so fast at the thought of a plastic bag he forgot to put his boots in the car. It was a great relief to learn that it was only colic, but we felt rather guilty watching him depart half an hour later — his evening spoilt, his suede shoes covered in mud and his light, off-duty trousers marked by

Annabel's flailing hooves as he felt hurriedly to find what was wrong.

He'd given her a morphia injection to ease the pain and told us to keep her on her feet and walk her about in the paddock. The danger with colic, he said, was the possibility of the gut getting twisted while she rolled. Otherwise, by the time the morphia wore off, the attack would have passed and she'd be all right.

She was indeed. The only trouble was, we hadn't been able to keep her on her feet. As the morphia took effect Annabel sank on the end of her halter like an anchor and went to sleep right in the middle of the paddock. We couldn't get her up again. We couldn't leave her, of course — just in case her gut did get twisted, or she failed to come round from the morphia, or one of the dozen or so other catastrophes we could think of occurred. So there we were. Me sitting in the field with her head on my lap. Charles enquiring every few minutes whether her breathing was all right. Donkeys get you like that. It didn't stop us realising, however — what with the decrepit state of the paddock, and people coming past and eyeing us curiously when they saw her stretched on out my lap like a scene from A *Midsummer Night's Dream,* and the thought that, for the umpteenth time, we'd got the Vet over at panic-point when it really wasn't serious at all — that our donkey hardly enhanced our social standing. Even though we wouldn't have parted with her for worlds.

A few weeks previously we'd had a fright because Annabel was limping. There was nothing in her foot when we looked, but, behind the hard rim of her hoof, the leathery part known as the frog looked soft and spongy to us. On one foot a bit of the frog actually appeared to be missing. Foot-rot, we diagnosed in alarm, remembering what a seaside donkey-man had once told us about not letting donkeys stand around on damp ground. In Ireland, he said, where they live in bogs so much, they often get soft spongy places on the bottom of their feet which can never be cured. The hoof just rots away and the donkey is fit for nothing but to be put down.

Filled with apprehension — there was a damp patch in Annabel's field and Charles said I *knew* he'd said often enough about bringing her in when it rained — we consulted Father Adams, who said it was undoubtedly foot-rot too, and I got straight on to the Vet. It had been a great relief on that occasion to find that it was only a sprained hock — *how* she'd sprained it when she hadn't been out of her paddock all day was a mystery known only to Annabel — but Mr Harler, having raced over after my call with visions of her feet disintegrating practically before his eyes, was a bit sharp about it.

He gave her cortisone to reduce the swelling. Advised us to keep her shut up for a couple of days so she couldn't walk on it too much. Let him know if the swelling didn't go down, of course, he said. But, if it wasn't too much to ask, he *would* like his Sunday in peace…

What happened certainly wasn't our fault. The previous winter we'd had a jennet called Henry over from the local seaside to keep Annabel company. Jennets, being a cross between a donkey and a horse, are not supposed to be able to mate, but Annabel and Henry had had a shot at it. With the local riding mistress as witness, as a matter of fact, after they'd broken out at two o'clock one morning and she'd found them running around in the road outside her stables. She put them in her paddock for the night and there, next morning, they'd mated. When she told us about it, saying but of course it was all right, jennets and mules were barren, weren't they, Charles recalled with alarm Henry's owner saying they were as a rule but he'd heard of a case or two in the East where they'd managed it, and we had something else to worry about.

For months we'd kept an eye on Annabel. Nothing had come of it, however. What with all the other exigencies of donkey-keeping and looking after Siamese cats we'd really quite forgotten about it. Until we shut Annabel into her shed in the paddock that weekend to rest her foot, and people came past and saw the hurdle door tied into place, and then — not having counted the months on their fingers as we had — the rumour went round the village that Annabel was having her foal.

We'd been out on the Saturday afternoon. When we came back the paddock was strewn with apples and cake. A large bag of bread was propped at the paddock gate. Another bag of bread and a box of sugar were at the kitchen door. That evening practically the entire village either called or telephoned to enquire after Annabel's health. And at ten o'clock the Vet rang up.

What was this about our donkey being in foal? he demanded. He sounded rather brusque for someone ringing up to congratulate us. Perhaps he was annoyed at not being told, I thought. Hastily I assured him that it wasn't true. If it had been, of course he'd have been the *first* to know, I told him consolingly.

First his foot, said Mr Harler. It was just that they didn't *give* cortisone to animals in foal. There could be all sorts of complications and it would be just like us not to know. When I explained that it was a false alarm — about people seeing her shed shut up and her romance the previous winter with Henry — he said that was just like us too. We certainly got no uplift from our donkey.

Two: So Do Siamese Cats

At first sight, of course, the cats more than made up for the prestige we lost over Annabel. People who would have passed the cottage with scarcely a glance stopped as if struck when they saw them in the yard. Solomon sitting tall and straight behind the fish-pool like a statue of Bast, eyeing them with the incomparable hauteur of a Siamese tom who knows how handsome he is. Sheba beaming cross-eyedly at them from her favourite spot on the coal-house roof. 'Oh look — Siamese!' they would exclaim, gazing with new eyes at this little valley cottage which, for all its apparent modesty, housed two such aristocrats of the cat world.

That was all they knew about it. Those elegant creatures, looking as if the only way they moved from place to place was in a royal litter with Charles and I carrying the poles, regularly got us into as much trouble as a posse of donkeys put together and were, just around then, involved in a feud with a black and white tom.

He was an immigrant from a neighbouring village.

People knew who his owners were and he'd been taken home to them several times with the suggestion that they have him neutered. Miss Wellington, a neighbour of ours who worried about these things, even offered to pay for it. His owners wouldn't hear of it. Apparently they liked a feline Captain Blood around the place. Old Butch wouldn't be the same if they did that, they said, fondling his black and white bullet head affectionately. Too right he wouldn't, and the valley would have been a far more peaceful place in consequence. As it was he'd be back within hours, looking up his girlfriends and fighting with the boys, and Charles and I, when we knew he was around, had to keep a non-stop watch on Solomon. Other cats, after one encounter, had a wholesome respect for Butch. Solomon, our black-faced Walter Mitty, had the idea that he, not Butch, was Captain Blood and was prepared to fight till he dropped to prove it.

Why a neutered Siamese — particularly one so gentle-natured as Solomon, who would kick heftily at my arm with his back legs in play and then, worried in case he'd hurt me, look at me anxiously with his deep blue eyes, and thereafter kick deliberately wide so as not to touch me, should have such designs to be a fighter was inexplicable, but there it was. As a kitten he'd defied, and had to be rescued from, practically every cat in the neighbourhood. As a cat his howls — as of someone being sawn in pieces and if we didn't hurry up we wouldn't have a Solomon at *all* — sent us haring up the valley invariably to find that it was the other cat who was cornered. Solomon was merely practising psychology; telling his opponent what he'd do to him if he dared to move an inch.

When Butch came on the scene, however, it was a different matter. Butch wasn't intimidated by Oriental war-songs and bushed-up tails and somebody walking sideways at him like a crab. Butch just pitched in and *fought*. To our amazement, Solomon fought back. He came home with bleeding ears, with scratches on his face, occasionally with blood on his sleek cream chest — it made no difference. The very next time he heard Butch's troubadour love-song filtering down the valley — so small and high-pitched compared with a Siamese voice that, as Charles so often said, you'd hardly think Butch had the wherewithal to *be* a tom if we hadn't seen him swaggering past in the wake of his song like a miniature Minoan bull — and Solomon was off.

Sheba, on the contrary, was in. In and watching, Rapunzel-like, from the safety of the hall window. Sheba had once been bitten on the tail by a tom. She'd had an abscess the size of a tangerine on her rear as a result and hadn't forgotten it — until the day we were sitting on the lawn having tea.

Solomon was in the vegetable garden, which we'd cased thoroughly for signs of Butch and decided was safe for a while. Sheba — we didn't know where she was, except that it wouldn't be far away. No bold adventuress was Sheba. No further than the garden wall and run if a strange cat spoke to you was our blue girl's motto for safety. So we finished our tea, and Charles lay back in his deck-chair and said 'Now for five minutes' relaxation' — which is a favourite saying of his and one usually guaranteed to set things moving like a depth-charge — and sure enough, no sooner had he said it than there was the sound of a tremendous catfight and round the corner, and on to the lawn, rolled what appeared to be a large fur comet. It was going so fast we couldn't distinguish its component parts, but we had no doubt as to who they were. We were up, leaping the flowerbeds, shouting 'Solomon!' at the top of our voices to let him know help was at hand and hoping Butch wouldn't hit him too hard before we got there, when the comet suddenly stopped. Butch was there all right — a cowering, chastened Butch, with his head flat to the ground to escape the flailing paws. But his opponent — we nearly dropped when we realised it — wasn't Solomon. It was Sheba. Caught, presumably, sun-bathing in the yard and determined to defend her virtue to the end. Even as we watched she drew back, landed him a right-hook bang on his nose, and Butch disappeared over the gate.

Sheba fled indoors to consider her shame. Solomon arrived as fast as his legs would carry him from the vegetable garden, enquiring which way did he go and what — sniffing interestedly at Sheba — had he Done? You'd think they'd be glad that after that Butch never darkened our yard again. But no. Half an hour later Sheba — having apparently thought it over and decided that Butch had been paying her a compliment — appeared sleekly purring through the kitchen door and went and sat on the back gatepost in case he wanted to see her again. What was more, any time after that she heard Butch's boy-soprano in the distance, instead of running into the house for safety she nearly fell over herself rushing out of it to stand on the post and crane her neck up the lane to see if she could see him. While Solomon sat night after night in the open drive gateway, waiting for Butch to come by so he could fight him and complaining loudly, every time we spoke to him, that Sheba had spoiled everything as usual and why we kept her he didn't know.

He was there, looking in the wrong direction as usual, the night Miss Wellington came past with a dog the size of an elephant and the dog, spotting Solomon, chased him playfully through a row of cloches. We were having supper at the time and the first we knew of it was the sudden appearance of Miss Wellington in the lane outside our front gate, wringing her hands and yelling something we couldn't hear because the windows were shut. When we opened them she was wailing 'He's not *my* dog! He's not *my* dog!' and when we rushed out to see what had happened, Solomon was on the woodshed roof with his leg bleeding; the dog — a mastiff, who, so his owner told us later, wouldn't harm a flea but the silly clot would try to play with cats — was streaking up the hill as if the devil was after him; the row of cloches over the strawberries was completely smashed; and there, still wringing her hands in the lane and saying he wasn't her dog, was Miss Wellington. She'd brought him for a walk out of kindness. Let him off his lead for a run out of kindness. According to Father Adams she'd let a camel off his lead in the Sahara out of kindness if she got the chance and a good thing Lawrence hadn't had *her* along on his expedition. And there were we, out of surgery hours again, ringing up the Vet to say Solomon had had an accident and please could we bring him over at once.

Mr Harler was very nice about it. Said Poor Little Man to Solomon and we'd soon have a couple of stitches in that. But as he worked away, with Charles and I holding Solomon and poor little Fatso looking pleadingly at us for assurance, as he always did at the Vet's, that we weren't going to leave him there, were we, honestly he was as good as new... 'Odd, isn't it', said Mr Harler musingly, 'that it's always your lot who get into trouble, and always at such peculiar times?'

Actually Solomon wasn't any more anxious to see him than he was to see Solomon. Some while previously we'd found Fatso sitting on the settee surreptitiously examining one of his paws, which was swollen like a fat brown boxing glove. A sting of some sort, obviously — but before we could get a look at it Solomon had seen us watching him and tucked it out of sight beneath him. Nothing wrong with him, he assured us airily — knowing from experience that if there was he was set for an immediate visit to the Vet's. Everything all right. All paws correct. He was just sitting there having a rest. The moment he thought we were out of sight, however, out came the paw again, with Solomon, who always worried about himself, looking at it anxiously, obviously wondering whether it was going to stay like that forever.

Oddly enough — or maybe not so oddly seeing that we were forever snatching him away from some grounded bee or wasp that he'd cornered in the garden and was either poking experimentally with his paw or about to eat when we belted up — not long after he was chased through the cloches he got stung again. On his chin this time. I was in the living-room when he dashed through the door, batted a stray piece of paper round the carpet, leapt to the top shelf of the bookcase and then, with a roar, to the back of my chair, where he poised like a ballet dancer with his tail raised demanding that I chase him … throw things for him … anything, yelled Solomon, to liven the place up and let a fit cat get a bit of exercise.

I wondered at his sudden exuberance. Even more so when I noticed the peculiarity of his profile. Fatso was getting a double chin. He must, I decided, be putting on weight…

Only later, by which time Solomon had enough chins for a dowager duchess but was still bounding determinedly about the place like a kitten, did I realise what had happened. Solomon had been stung, and this sudden display of athletics was to put us off. To conceal the fact that his chin was swelling, or, if we did happen to notice it, to convince us that it was nothing. Just a trick of our imagination. No need, on any account, for anybody to call the Vet.

Nobody did. His chin went down again. His leg, after the episode with the mastiff, healed perfectly. Just to prove it he had a fight with a large ginger tom he found sitting in the yard one day, who forthwith went up the garden like a rocket and was last seen three feet in the air outside the garage, with Solomon up there with him, kicking him in the stomach as they went — and then it was September, and we went on holiday.

Usually we went to the Mediterranean, to lie in the sun and relax after a year of arduous endeavour. That year, thanks to our dear little donkey, we went horse-riding. In the rain, in the wilds of Scotland.

The thing was, people were always coming past the cottage with horses. Sometimes the horses liked Annabel and refused to go on till they'd put their heads over her fence and had a word with her. Sometimes they were afraid of her and we had to go out and help their owners get them past. Either way, sooner or later we got talking to their riders and they assumed that if we were donkey-minded we must be horse-minded — which we were to a degree, but not to the extent of actually getting upon one and *riding* it.

Before we knew where we were, however, one or two of them had mentioned that any time we wanted to ride we might like to help exercise their horses — perhaps little Annabel could come too, they said, with a pat on her buff Beatle fringe — and there we were. Carried away by a vision of ourselves on a couple of show-jumpers, far across the hills, with Annabel, her minute golden mane flying in the breeze, galloping at our sides... Oh yes, we said. We'd *love* to.

Fortunately I had enough sense to say we were rather busy at the moment and could we leave it till after the holidays. Privately I said to Charles that, not having been on a horse for nearly twenty years, if I *was* going to fall off it was going to be miles from the village — not somewhere where Father Adams would immediately appear round a corner to enquire whether my backside was sore, or Miss Wellington go shrieking up the lane that I was dead and it wasn't her fault.

So that was how we came to go to Scotland. To a place where, for a solid week, we could ride, look after the horses ourselves (if we exercised them for people, said Charles, we should also know how to feed and groom them — not just ride them and hand them over to someone else as we'd done in our youth at riding school), and at the end of it, we hoped, we'd be fighting fit. Ready to ride anything. Galloping along the lanes with a touch of our riding hats to Father Adams and a nonchalant wave to Miss Wellington...

Which was how, by Tuesday afternoon, we came to be sheltering in a wet Scottish wood. Aching in every muscle. Soaked to the skin. And dealing, by way of holiday relaxation, with another case of colic.

It was my pony Pixie who was the patient. Charles leading her up and down while I held his mount, a horse the size of a battle charger who was appropriately called Warrior. Pixie — a grey Highland pony not much larger than Annabel and with, from what I had seen of her, much the same temperament — was groaning, rolling her eyes and leaning heavily on Charles with an air of not having long to live.

With our usual optimism it occurred to us that perhaps she hadn't. It was only our diagnosis that it was colic. She wasn't our pony. We were miles from a Vet. We had never been wetter in our lives...

Had it, panted Charles, struggling determinedly to hold up Pixie while Pixie strove equally determinedly to sink to the ground and get her gut twisted... Had it occurred to me that this was the result of owning that donkey?

Three: To Horse! To Horse!

As a matter of fact it had been occurring to me ever since we arrived at the riding centre the previous weekend. After dinner on Saturday night for a start, when, instead of the drink in some small Continental cafe with which we usually celebrated the first night of our holiday, we sat in a circle in the harness room with a dozen other eager beavers, industriously tying knots.

Tethering knots. We might not have heard of them on those dear little jaunts of our youth, said the instructor, but if we didn't learn how to do them now, sooner or later we'd find ourselves legging it back from a twenty-mile ride on which we'd lost our horses while we stopped for sandwiches.

Charles, being all keen and eager at this stage, got so enthusiastic that long after I was in bed that night he was still tying tethering knots with his shoelace round the back of a bedroom chair. Hardly able to wait to be galloping over the hills, tethering his horse to a tree when he felt like it while he stopped for a snack from his saddle bag, he was, to the astonishment of the maid who brought up the tea, up and practising them again before seven the next morning.

It was the last time our turret bedroom in that old Scottish castle saw Charles prancing happily around it at that hour of day. Holding his back and groaning, yes... Complaining because it was his turn to take the water buckets round the stables before breakfast and, according to Charles, if he made it down the turret staircase without dislocating his spine his legs would never stand the strain of the buckets anyway ... but never again so light-heartedly. Two hours after untying his final practice knot with a flourish and assuring me that there was nothing to it, it was all coming back to him, Charles was up on Warrior discovering that, after an interval of twenty years, there was a great deal to it indeed. Mostly the bumping.

One never loses the rhythm of the trot, of course. Five minutes on that first morning's road run and the entire cavalcade was, out of the dim recesses of its memory, rising and sitting automatically to the instructor's ringing call of 'Hup Down, Hup Down, Hup Down, Hup Down'. Five minutes more, alas, and we were all back to bumping like sacks of turnips. What we *had* lost was the ability of our leg muscles to get us up and down in the peculiarly English style of riding which, for those who had never experienced it, can best be compared to crouching on a hassock, legs apart, rising and sitting inexorably to a metronome set at sixty ticks to the minute, with the prospect of getting slapped on a tight-trousered bottom with the force of a carpet beater if you come down at the wrong moment.

Charles, considering it red-faced and jolting from the back of Warrior, said we must have been mad. He'd never live to tie a tether-knot, he announced between gasps. Any moment now he was going to fall off and break his neck.

That Charles was able to talk at all was due to the fact that he *was* on Warrior. A big horse trots at an easier pace than a pony. I, jiggering along at his side on Pixie, who took at least two trots to keep up with Warrior's one, was going up and down like a cocktail shaker. Any time I tried to say anything, my teeth rattled.

That was a soul-searching morning, if ever there was one.

Rising to the trot till we could rise no longer. Bouncing for the next few minutes with the feeling of being slapped on the bottom by a frying pan. Roused at nightmarish intervals by the instructor's cry of 'Car coming, everybody! Don't let 'em see you lagging now. Come on — HUP Down! HUP Down! HUP Down! HUP Down!' At which we all obediently hupped like a troop of Household Cavalry and practically died in our saddles as soon as the car had passed.

It was a soul-searching afternoon, too. After lunch we dragged ourselves back on to those horses and, under the relentless eye of the instructor, practised cantering. Three people fell off and the only reason I didn't was that I was cheating. I happen to have long arms. Sitting deceptively upright, keeping ahead of everybody else so they couldn't see what I was up to, quietly I was clinging to the saddle like a leech.

I ached. I longed to die. At the beginning of every canter the saddle rose, as I grabbed at it, with a lurch that practically lifted Pixie from the ground. But I didn't fall off. As a reward for which, after we'd watered the horses that evening, and fed them and groomed them and massaged their backs to loosen their muscles (nobody, I noticed with sudden self-sympathy, was worrying about loosening mine), the instructor announced that I was one of the selected few who would be permitted to ride the eight horses who spent their nights out at grass across the river — as against the six who slept in to give us the experience of cleaning out their stables — down to their grazing ground *bareback*.

There was just no end to that perishing day. There being no way out short of confessing, the next thing I knew I was on Pixie's naked back jolting agonisingly down the road. Smiling brightly, of course. Studying the scenery with nonchalant interest as I went — the stables, the group of elms by the paddock gate, the colourful lichen-covered wall that bordered the track down to the river. And privately wondering whether I'd be carried back past it on a stretcher.

Charles had been selected for bareback riding, too. But Charles, apart from his stiffness, *was* a rider. It was coming back to him indeed. He rode his horse like a show-jumper now, down the track to the ford, across it, touched his heels to Warrior's sides, and was up the almost perpendicular bank on the other side as if he was flying. I, following behind him, was inspired by the sight of this to touch my heels to Pixie's sides too, and the next thing I knew, I was in the river. Straight over her tail I slid, but nobody was worrying about me. Just everybody, including Charles, shouting that I shouldn't have let go of her reins and racing after her in case they tripped her up.

Things even themselves out, of course. That evening — stiff but convinced that his aches were only temporary; forgetting the setbacks of the day and remembering only the ecstasy of that surge up the river bank — Charles volunteered for seven o'clock duty next morning at the stables.

'This is the life,' he said enthusiastically as we went to bed. The smell of the good old straw. The feel of a good old horse between one's knees. A night's rest to get rid of his stiffness and he'd probably be up at six and go down to ride Warrior *up* from the river fields bareback as well.

Alas for the visions which, in one form or another, dawn perpetually on Charles's horizons. By the time he'd had a night's rest his muscles had seized up completely. He did get down to the stables — groaning and muttering at every turn of the turret steps that we were paying for this and why the hell didn't they have stable boys. And he returned at breakfast time to announce that one of the good old horses (only he didn't call them that this time) had stepped on his foot.

One of the smaller ponies, fortunately, and, having had experience with Annabel, he'd *almost* got his foot out in time. She'd only got him on the toe. She had shoes on, nevertheless. We discussed Charles's toe during the whole of breakfast.

It all worked out in the end, though. Monday was hell. Tuesday — the day Pixie got colic — our bruises came out and I found the insides of my legs were black from knees to ankles and I couldn't wear nylons for a week. By Wednesday, however, we were all of us back in form. We rode on long excursions through the countryside. It was raining still, but we lit fires and ate our lunch around them and enjoyed the feeling of trotting, ruddyfaced, back to tea past weaker mortals sheltering in their cars. We rose to the trot now, too, with the ease of oiled pistons, and sang as we trotted with no thought of breathlessness, and discussed the merits of our horses as if we'd owned them for years.

Charles was particularly lyrical about Warrior. One morning we'd been riding across a moor, with nobody apparently in view for miles, when just as he leaned down to open a gate a shepherd suddenly appeared on the other side of the wall. Warrior, never having seen anybody at that particular spot in his life before, promptly bolted, and Charles, caught leaning half out of his saddle, was hard put to it for a minute or two to get control of him. Just like Cossack riding it was, the way he pulled himself up in the saddle, reined Warrior gradually to a halt and then, wheeling in his tracks, brought him trotting back to the rest of us. The instructor held this up to us as an example — how not to lose our heads and to keep tight control with hands and knees — but Charles attributed it all to Warrior. It was wonderful how that horse responded, he said. There was real understanding between him and Warrior. He wouldn't mind taking him home with us.

When Charles uses that expression my heart sinks. I like animals too, but I have never felt impelled to consider building a pond on the front lawn so that I could keep a King Penguin (this after a visit to the Zoo at which Charles spent an entranced three-quarters of an hour watching one of them doing all the smaller penguins out of their fish). I have never had the bright idea that a camel would be an ideal companion for Annabel on the grounds that (discounting the fact that Annabel is a Scandinavian variety) camels and donkeys are companion creatures of the East and Charles once knew a very intelligent one in Egypt. But I have had the task of talking Charles out of these and various similar ideas, and a pretty narrow squeak it has been on some occasions.

In the case of the horses it was, I must agree, somewhat different. If it came to that, I wouldn't have minded taking Pixie home for myself. It was practically the end of the riding season; the horses *were* lent out for the winter in exchange for their keep if people wanted them; and for all Pixie's wilfulness and her habit of stumping stolidly along on the way home saying she was tired — until, on the advice of the instructor, I swung my riding crop thoughtfully on the end of my finger as I rode, whereupon Pixie immediately leapt into a trot saying Goodness Gracious Her, almost asleep she'd been and why hadn't I woken her up … for all that, her nodding little head and sturdy fat grey body were beginning to grow on me.

The snag — which I could see, but Charles, in his sudden affection for Warrior, stubbornly refused to do — was that while it might be all right for people in the neighbourhood to take Warrior or Pixie or Morven and feed and ride them through the winter, *we* lived four hundred miles away.

How were we going to get them home? I enquired. 'Ride them,' said Charles, at which I had a vision of ourselves trotting determinedly down through the Potteries and Birmingham and arriving home somewhere around Christmas. 'Put them on the train,' he said airily, when I said but if we rode them how would we get the car home. Despite my insistence that that would cost a fortune — and we'd have to send them back next May and that would cost a fortune too, let alone the fact that by that time we'd probably decide we couldn't part with them and have to buy them and where on earth would we keep them permanently — despite all that Charles still went on talking about taking Warrior home, and telling Warrior how he was going to enjoy himself down in the West Country on all those pony nuts Charles was going to buy him ... when fate, as it usually does if one waits long enough, took a hand.

We rode twenty miles on the Friday, and on the last lap of the run home it rained. Solid Highland rain that ran off the roads in rivers, and soaked our saddles, and steamed like sauna baths off the horses' backs. We got back to the stables. Watered and fed our charges. Charles, damp but determined, prepared to mount Warrior bareback for his nightly trek down to the river fields...

Warrior was such a big horse that not even Charles, who is six feet tall, could mount him bareback from the ground. Instead he used a convenient bank of earth at the side of the stable yard as a mounting block, and — as Warrior, understanding or not, immediately moved as far away as his reins would permit — Charles had to jump at him sideways from there.

This time — it was as simple as that — as Charles prepared to jump, his heels slid down the rain-soaked surface of the earth-heap and he landed on his back. He hadn't fallen off. He hadn't even got as far as actually jumping. He'd strained his back though, and it was obvious that he wasn't going to be able to ride for a while, so we came back from Scotland, after all, without Pixie or Charles's friend Warrior.

Nothing, when we got back, could shake Father Adams's conviction that Charles had fallen off his horse. He kept reminiscing about how Lawrence had fallen off his camel when he was learning to ride. Miss Wellington kept asking Charles how his back was and telling me that she hoped I didn't mind her saying it but wasn't he perhaps a little old for such pursuits? Charles himself alternated between saying that he'd show them in a week or two whether he could ride or not and then coming in, bent like Father Time after a bout of log-cutting, announcing that he was crippled for life.

He proved that he wasn't three days after we got back from Scotland, when he had to go up a tree in a hurry to rescue Solomon.

Four: Solomon and the Loch Ness Monster

What happened was that we'd come home late from town, put on all the outside lights, and let the cats out for a look round while we fed Annabel and put the car away.

We kept a strict eye on them as we did our chores, knowing Solomon's propensity for looking one minute as if he was glued to the fish-pool wall for life and the next being half-way up the lane apparently *en route* for Siam. So when, ten minutes after we'd let them out, we went to get them in again and discovered that Solomon, who five seconds before had been peering suspiciously down a mouse-hole in the rockery, was now nowhere to be seen, we didn't take it seriously at first.

We looked over the front gate, over the side gate, inside the coalhouse... We looked in the potting shed, where there was a heap of sand which Solomon sometimes fancied as a change from his earth-box. There was a rat-hole in the hard-packed sand. We'd once seen Solomon sit hopefully beside it for a while and then, becoming bored and deciding that nobody was coming out today, he'd dug a hole of his own in front of the first one and sat on it, his mind obviously by now on other things, his innocent little bottom exposed to attack in a way that turned us cold when we thought of it, but that was Solomon all over.

He wasn't on the sand-heap now, though. Neither was he up the lane in the ruined cottage, or sitting thinking on the wall of Annabel's house, or — we were beginning to get desperate by this time — locked by accident in Father Adams's outside lavatory, which we checked by tiptoeing up his path and looking in.

I called him — 'Tollywollywolly' in the yodel up and down the valley that I knew, even as I did it, would have the neighbours tapping their foreheads and saying how sorry they felt for Charles, but at least it always brought an answering wail from Solomon, to let me know where he was and would I please hurry up and fetch him.

Not this time it didn't. There was only complete silence and the terrible conviction, after we'd ranged the valley for nearly two hours with torches, and shouted till our throats were sore, that a fox must have taken him. How, we couldn't imagine. The lights were on, the doors were open, we'd kept check on him every minute or so and the idea of Solomon, who always had so much to say about everything, being carried off from under our noses without so much as a peep from that world-shattering voice of his was unbelievable.

But there it was. Twelve o'clock. Nearly two hours of searching for him, and now we had to admit that he'd gone. At which point, standing miserably on the lawn, worn completely to a standstill, I shone my torch up into the damson tree by the front gate, and there he was. A faint dark shadow a few feet from the top. His eyes glittering fixedly in the torchlight. So unmoving that — my next mental crisis of the evening — I was certain he must be dead.

He'd fallen from a higher branch, I decided. He never could climb anyway. Another cat must have chased him, and he'd slipped and been transfixed on a sharp lower branch, which was why, in all those long hours when we'd passed and re-passed under the tree, only a few yards from the house, he hadn't answered us…

At that point my knees gave way. It was Charles who rushed for the garage, moved the car and, despite his back, raced back down the garden with the fruit ladder. But the fruit ladder wasn't long enough, and when we called and reached with encouraging hands from only inches below, there was still no move from the motionless form above us. I died a thousand deaths while Charles raced up the garden, fetched the double roof ladders without even stopping to separate them, thrust them up into the tree and was up there, in seconds, with our seal man. I died a further one, too, with relief, when he said that Solomon was alive — apparently unharmed, except that he appeared to be in a coma — and handed him, limp as a little black waterlily, down into my waiting arms.

What frightened him we never knew. My theory is that it was a badger. A fox I think he would have taken for a dog. But a badger — and there are badger setts just a little way down the valley, and we often hear them grunting their way through the woods at night, but so far as we knew Solomon himself had never seen one … a badger, six times the size of himself, coming down the lane with that great white stripe down its head like a witch-doctor and encountered, perhaps, right at our very gate as Solomon nipped over for an airing … that would have frightened him all right.

Charles said it was either that or we'd brought the Loch Ness monster home in the car-boot. Whichever it was, Solomon bolted upstairs as soon as we got him indoors and remained there for three whole days. He ate up there. He lived up there. It would be wrong to say that he slept up there because for three days solid, so far as we could tell, Solomon didn't sleep at all.

Every time we went into the hall a small black face scanned us anxiously from the landing like a defender at the Siege of York looking down from a portcullis. When we went upstairs he peered worriedly round our legs as we got to the top, to make sure the enemy hadn't crept up behind us. He wouldn't look out of a window at all. Presumably that would have given away the fact that he was in our bedroom. And when we peered cautiously out ourselves — the feeling of being besieged having spread itself to us by this time, the way he was carrying on — Solomon hid under the bed.

He apparently was up there for good. Sheba, with true Siamese contrariness, was meanwhile going further afield than she ever did normally. Every time we looked for her she seemed to be either vanishing over the front gate or setting off up the path through the woods — so much the innocent little lamb going out as tiger bait that, even as we ran to fetch her back to safety, we wondered, knowing Sheba, whether she was doing it deliberately.

It was a great relief when, at the end of three days, Solomon appeared once more in the living room and, after watching Sheba carefully for an hour or two, satisfied himself that she was indeed — no fooling — going right out into the garden and coming back in one piece. Following which, the next time she went out he went out behind her. It was even more of a relief when a week or so later a neighbour who lived beyond us up the lane reported something he'd seen on his way home one night in his car. Coming down the hill he was, he said, and there in his headlights, standing by her paddock gate, was Annabel — and beneath her, glowing oddly in the darkness, were three pairs of disembodied green eyes. Stopping to investigate, with his headlights full on the fence, he'd discovered that there were three cats sitting under her. One was his own cat, Rufus. Another was the black and white cat from up the lane. And the third was the ginger stray Solomon had fought before the holidays.

They were sheltering from the rain, he said. They looked as if they were in conference. And Annabel was standing over them with an air of great importance.

This reassured us on two counts. That there couldn't be anything really dangerous in the valley, otherwise these other cats — far more wordly-wise than Solomon, for all his air of being Lord of the Valley and Anybody Want To Dispute It — wouldn't have been there. And that Annabel — our hearts warmed with pleasure when we thought of it — liked cats.

We'd never been quite sure about this. True we'd once seen her nudging Sheba playfully along with her nose — Sheba turning to natter at her over her shoulder as she went and the pair of them acting like a friendship scene out of Walt Disney. We'd also, however, on several occasions, caught her chasing Solomon in the nearest thing we'd seen to real-life Cowboys and Indians — and whether Solomon's big bat ears were streamlined for the fun of it, or because he thought avoidance of wind-resistance was his only hope in his present extremity, we never knew. He'd be back sitting in her paddock within half an hour, but that was Solomon all over. Annabel would most likely be grazing peacefully a yard away as though she'd now decided Siamese cats were some sort of butterfly and the worst that the big-eared seal one could do was sit on her cow-parsley — but that was Annabel all over too. We just didn't know.

Three cats, though — sitting under her where one stamp of her hoof could do so much damage and all Annabel did was stand there like a benevolent mother sheep keeping the rain off … that showed what she was like, we said. And when a night or two later we found she was actually allowing the ginger stray to share her house with her, we were even more impressed.

Annabel was very jealous of her house. Solomon and Sheba weren't allowed to enter it at all. We ourselves were allowed to go in with food and bedding, but once the food was down Annabel stood possessively over it and offered to kick us soundly if we touched one bit of hay. She marked it for all the world to know as hers by standing straddle-legged in front of it, whenever she returned from a walk, and spending a penny. And if we wanted more proof than that of the importance to Annabel of Annabel's house, we had it in her behaviour the day we took her to the County Show. Sixty miles she went by horsebox, to collect for charity, and a full day it was indeed.

She rode regally in the big double horsebox that had been lent to us as though she'd been used to it all her life, though in fact it was the first time she'd ever been in one. She emerged from it, when we got to the showground, as if she were the Horse of the Year arriving at the White City. She did her rounds with her collecting box with the mixture of modesty and self-assurance that we knew of old was Annabel being a Lady, and was photographed and petted, and watched the horses, when we led her to the railings of the show-ring, with an intentness that signified she knew just as well as we did what they were doing there — *and* had her own ideas as to which horses were doing it properly.

Twelve hours solid she'd been away by the time she stepped down from the horse box again and into her paddock. And what did she do, this donkey of ours who for once had behaved as a status symbol should and there were probably misguided people all over the county that very minute saying wasn't she a poppet, and what about one themselves, as a playmate for the children? Straight into her house she went. Spending a penny on the way, of course, by way of relief and to let the rabbits know that Annabel was back. When we went in a few minutes later with her supper and her water-bucket, though this was summer and it was still light and warm outside,

Annabel was lying down. Resting, we gathered. After the strain of her public appearance. In the privacy of her Home.

For Annabel, a couple of months later, to invite the ginger stray to share her home was really something indeed. Charles discovered it one night when he went out to feed her. Her house had been constructed for quickness, when we first had her, out of a small, roofless stone shed, lined with hurdles to give it height, with a sloping roof of corrugated iron lashed to metal poles, and with a further hurdle as a door. This arrangement was so successful that we'd left it like that — the only deterioration being that the hurdles had warped slightly, and in places were not now flat with the walls.

It was behind one of these that the cat was lying, in the gap between the hurdle and the wall. Curled into a ball.

Strategically placed so that, while Annabel couldn't step on him, when she lay down to sleep (Annabel was a creature of habit and always lay in exactly the same position) he was right where she'd breathe on him, acting as a sort of fan heater through the night.

He lay there unmoving, obviously wondering whether Charles would turn him out and ready to fly if he did. Charles pretended not to see him. Annabel ate her supper innocently — also pretending not to see him but Charles said she had that complacent pout to her mouth which we knew so well, and which in this case indicated that she knew something we didn't, and that Annabel was feeling Benevolent.

She was so benevolent that two nights later the cat ventured out from behind the hurdle and began to sleep in an even warmer place. Right against her head. We knew this because there was a deep indentation in the straw where she slept, and when we went out in the mornings now the cat was lying, still curled into a ball, against the place where her head had been.

The next thing Charles reported was that he'd seen Annabel and her new friend eating side by side from her bowl of breakfast bread. Had I, enquired Charles, any old food Solomon and Sheba didn't want? A cat had to be pretty hungry to eat bread, and though Annabel might think she was being generous, he couldn't be getting much nourishment out of that.

So the ginger stray, now known as Robertson on account of his marmalade colouring, was put on the strength. He got two meals a day — taken up to him in Annabel's house because Solomon and Sheba wouldn't have stood for our feeding him in the cottage. Milk — at which he purred his delight like an orphan being taken into a rich man's house and given the delicacies he'd so long seen only with his nose pressed to the window. He was unwise, actually, to make such a song about the milk. Annabel, thinking it must be something special to warrant all that noise, promptly forgot her good intentions, pushed him to one side, and drank it herself. Annabel as a foal had indignantly refused to drink the cow's milk we offered her, declaring that we were poisoning her and it wasn't like Mum's. The sight of her now, delicately pursing her lips into a saucer of it like a dowager duchess taking tea, in order to show Robertson that everything round there was hers, was absolutely typical.

Robertson was a match for her, though. A few intrusions like that and Robertson, when she stuck her big white nose into his saucer, sat up and slapped her on it. A spectacular left and right which, oddly enough, Annabel didn't appear to mind in the least. If our two had done it to her they'd have gone through the doorway like a couple of shooting stars. When Robertson did it, all she did was snort to show she didn't want his old milk anyway, and go back to eating her hay.

They slept together. They fed together. When anybody called to see Annabel at her paddock gate Robertson's little ginger figure was there as well, and as they fondled her head Robertson rubbed against her legs and rose, purring, on his own hind legs to share in the petting. The amazing thing was that Annabel — so jealous when the jennet was with us that she pushed between him and visitors and kicked him if anybody so much as spoke to him — didn't mind at all. Maybe, knowing Annabel, because she thought she'd put one over on us. Adopted him herself. Been really clever and slipped him in when we weren't looking.

The only ones who did object were Solomon and Sheba. Robertson, realising that for all we fed him in Annabel's stable the food actually came up the path from the cottage, started coming to meet us when we took it up. Sometimes he waited on the wall by the garage. Sometimes he appeared through the door of the conservatory, where he'd apparently been looking for mice to fill in time. One day, to Solomon's intense indignation, he appeared on the path outside our window while we were still at breakfast and sat there looking expectantly in at us while Solomon howled at him from inside to go away. All the Food round here was his. And all the Scraps were SHEBA'S, roared Solomon, his voice rising in indignant crescendo at the sight of Robertson, taking no notice of him at all, but still sitting there looking expectant.

Even after we'd escorted Robertson back to the paddock with the dish of food for which he'd come, Solomon still wouldn't be content. He sniffed the wall by the garage and sprayed it to mark the boundary. He sniffed the path where Robertson had sat, and sprayed the nearby jasmine by way of warning. He sniffed round the flower pots in the conservatory and sprayed those, according to Charles who'd witnessed it, like a Whirling Dervish with a hose pipe.

Solomon, of course, had been spraying outdoor landmarks to mark his ownership ever since his delighted discovery that, neuter or not, he *could* spray. What really brought home to us the seriousness with which our two regarded Robertson's arrival was the behaviour of Sheba, whom I also found sniffing intently one day in the conservatory. Not to worry, I said, stroking her delicate little ears as she looked up at me. Robertson wasn't going to live with us. It was only Solomon being Silly, I said — and laughed to feel her stand, as she had a habit of doing when she wanted to show special closeness to us, on my feet.

It was a good thing I was wearing gum-boots. When I looked down she was determinedly spraying a chrysanthemum plant — and the lot, this being her first attempt ever at direction and I hadn't, until that moment, known that female cats were capable of spraying at all — was going straight over my legs.

She wasn't Worrying, said Sheba when she'd finished her personal contribution to the defence preparations. She and Solomon were keeping him off.

Five: The Bread Line

There are various indications of the approach of winter in the village. The emergence of Miss Wellington in a fur hat, for example, and the appearance at Father Adams's windows of a set of maroon plush curtains which, having belonged to his grandmother and looking it, have a psychologically depressing effect on everybody save Father Adams himself for the next six months.

That particular year, however, it was the behaviour of the rooks that aroused the greatest comment around the place. Based a good half-mile away in the elms around the Rectory, with a birds' eye view of Farmer Pursey's cornfield and consequently rarely seen in our part of the world, they had suddenly taken to flying down the valley in formation in the mornings. And the thing that made everybody notice them was that one of them talked so much as he flew. Not cawing, but chattering away to his companions like an incorrigible gossip on a village bus.

We wondered whether it was the rook that, years before, had been raised as a fledgling by Father Adams's grandson, Timothy, and used to chatter to people as they passed the gate. Whether it was or not, his nattering as he accompanied the flight down the valley caused people to look up, and so, by force of country habit, did his nattering on the flight back. It was on the return flight, however, that the onlookers stood open-mouthed and stared. When they came back the entire armada of rooks — including the natterer, still talking indefatigably away but rather more muffled this time because his mouth was full — were carrying pieces of bread Charles and I recognised the source of the phenomenon the moment we saw it, of course. Annabel. The cook in Charles's favourite lunching place, who insisted on presenting him with a bag of bread crusts for her every day, had, as winter approached, increased the supply on the ground that the dear little soul could do with a bit of feeding now the colder weather was coming. The dear little soul, filled to bursting point with hay and pony nuts, couldn't encompass another crumb. Most of it was lying uneaten in her bowl now that Robertson was getting proper cat food. There weren't even any rats about to eat it, thanks to Robertson himself, who kept leaving large fat dead ones in the path just to show us what a handy cat we'd taken on. And so — no doubt with the same Big-Eared Lady Bountiful expression on her face that she used when patronising Robertson. Annabel was letting the rooks have it.

Charles didn't like to say anything to the cook for fear of offending her. She, enthusiastically doing her good turn for the winter, went on stepping up supplies to the point where he was coming home every night with two large carrier bags overflowing with bread-crusts. Even the rooks couldn't cope with that lot, of course and, as inexorably as things always happen with us, eventually we reached a state where we were running round after dark tipping bagfuls of it over hedges, near foxholes and badger setts — anywhere where we felt something might be glad to eat it, yet far enough away not to encourage rats or foxes near the cottage.

In the end, after several occasions on which we were caught in the headlights of neighbours' cars either having just ditched a bagful over a hedge and trying to look innocent, or with the bag clutched like loot in Charles's arms and our looking extremely guilty, he just had to explain to the cook before we got ourselves arrested.

She, without curtailing his own meals by way of retribution as Charles had apparently feared, agreed to cut down supplies. There was still enough bread for the rooks, and the natterer, who returned on his own at odd times during the day, could always find a spare piece or two to talk to himself about as he flew contentedly up the valley. A happy situation indeed, and there was nothing at all to worry Charles as he went out one day, with the idea of winter activities in mind, and bought a lathe he'd seen advertised in the paper.

For wood-turning it was, and it was worked by treadle, and Charles wasn't the least deterred by the owner explaining that he was selling it on his doctor's advice because one of his legs was longer than the other as a result of too much treadling and he was switching to an electric model. The seller was only twenty. He — Charles — was older and had stopped growing, said Charles when I pointed out the possibility of one of his legs getting longer too. It couldn't happen to *him*.

So, the following Saturday morning, the young man arrived towing the lathe in a box-shaped trailer through the swirling fog. Charles, who'd been feeding Annabel, came hurrying down to meet him and in his haste didn't tie up Annabel's gate. He and the young man bent over the trailer to unfasten the lathe and the young man commented on what an isolated place we lived in. Didn't go much for the country himself, he said. Gave him the willies it did, particularly in this sort of weather.

At that point there was a tapping of hooves in the lane, a donkey appeared apparently supernaturally through the fog, and the young man had the willies in earnest. Even when we explained about Annabel — that she'd pushed her gate open and come to see what was going on and that standing there looking accusingly at us from under her fringe didn't mean that she was going to bite anybody ... merely that she was letting us know she'd caught up with us — he still wasn't reassured. A lonely, fog-bound cottage. A donkey wandering the place like a Newfoundland dog. It obviously wouldn't have surprised him if we'd taken to our broomsticks at any moment. After delivering the least possible instruction on the vagaries of the lathe — even that with one eye over his shoulder in case there was anything behind him — he was off back to civilisation like a shot.

I could have done with a broomstick that afternoon. After lunch Charles put Annabel back in her paddock, came down to get her some hay, went into the woodshed *en route* for a quick look at his beloved lathe, and the next thing I knew, he was treadling happily away oblivious of anything, while Annabel — Charles having once more forgotten to fasten her gate — was again wandering happily along the lane.

Round the corner she went, past the cottage, through the Forestry gate and up the track towards the moor, with me in hot pursuit. Charles, engaged in a particularly intriguing piece of wood-turning, said he'd be with me in a second. Annabel, obviously feeling like a successful suffragette after getting out twice in one day and nobody was going to put *her* back in her paddock until she felt like it — kept me at bay all the way up the track with Pankhurst-like kicks. And at the top, where there was a field whose gate somebody had obligingly left open, she went in.

Easy, you may say. Shut the gate (which I did) and you've got your donkey. But she is a very fast donkey and it was a twenty-acre field. We began with Annabel pulling nonchalantly at a tuft of grass and then raising her head to study the view across to Wales. I crept quietly up behind her and, just as I stretched out my hand, Annabel decided the view was better a couple of yards away and strolled innocently across to look at it from there. We continued with the pair of us rambling round the field seemingly oblivious of each other and my making sudden dashes at her. At this Annabel made corresponding dashes, this time looking sideways at me as she ran with her head raised, which is the donkey equivalent of hearty laughter. Eventually I threw subterfuge to the wind and started to run after her openly — a mistake which ended with Annabel twenty acres away and me flat on my face over a furrow.

It was cold. It was getting dark. Annabel obviously had every intention of staying there all night — though if I had left her there and gone home Annabel's howls about there being ghosts up there and somebody fetch her home at once would, as I knew from experience, have rent the valley like a dinosaur. I got her in the end by climbing over the field fence into a coppice and pretending to study the undergrowth. Annabel immediately came and stuck her head over the fence to see what I was doing. I, bent to the ground, pottered disarmingly away from her. Annabel snorted to indicate where she thought people like me should be kept and moved away to graze in the field — with her back towards me to express disinterest but near enough for a front-row view in case I went completely bonkers — and I nipped stealthily back over the fence and grabbed her by the tail.

We took off then like John Gilpin's ride to York. Across the field we went, I hanging on like the tail end of a kite, till I realised I'd never stop her standing up. The only thing was to sit down — the way I stopped her when she was going too fast on her halter and sitting down, holding the rope with both hands, had the effect of suddenly dropping anchor.

I couldn't sit down holding her tail, however. It wasn't long enough. I had visions of it coming off in my hand. The ground was so muddy I didn't fancy being dragged across it on the seat of my pants, anyway, so I compromised by squatting. This resulted in Annabel slowing down but still making headway, and my following along in her wake as if I was doing a Cossack dance. The thought of what this must look like, up there in that lonely field at dusk, reduced me to such helpless laughter that Annabel stopped eventually from sheer astonishment. She looked round at me, still clinging to the end of her tail, snorted to indicate that if I was still there after that lot she might as well give in, and allowed me to work myself hand over hand along her back and put her halter on.

Well over an hour we'd been, but time means nothing to the craftsman. Charles was still treadling blissfully away when we got back. Another five minutes and he was coming to help me, he assured me. But he *knew* I wouldn't have any trouble...

Fortunately, before Charles's treadling leg grew as long as a stork's — as it must surely have done, over twenty-one or not, with all the practice he put in on the lathe in the next few weeks — winter set in early that year, and as it became too cold to work in the woodshed some of his initial enthusiasm wore off.

It was obvious there was something special about that winter. One afternoon we were bringing Annabel down a neighbouring valley at dusk and such an upsurge of birds flew up from the bushes as we passed — fieldfares resting in their hundreds on their migratory flight south — that Annabel, the rest of the winter, said there were ghosts along there and refused to go that way after dusk. A few nights later we were taking the cats for a walk by moonlight in our own valley and the same thing happened. One moment all was stillness and silver and shadow, and the next, up went such a rush of fieldfares they must have been roosting fifty to a tree. The cats, surprisingly, took no notice at all. Perhaps, with memories of little birds they'd ambushed singly in the past, they thought it wiser to pretend this army didn't exist. Not by so much as a twitch of her ears did Sheba show recognition, while Solomon, marching like a Colonel at the head of his troops through the Khyber Pass, looked neither to right nor to left.

Exist it did, though. Four days it took for the fieldfares, in such numbers as we'd never seen before, to clear our part of the country. 'Twas the sign of a long hard winter, said Father Adams sagely. And a long hard winter it was too — though not for a while yet. It didn't snow till Christmas. Which was why, that year, we didn't have a Christmas tree. A week before Christmas we had such a fine, sunny Sunday that we took our status symbol through the Forestry estate for an afternoon walk. At that time of year the Commission organises night patrols on its estates, to guard against gangs coming out from town with lorries to steal trees in bulk for the Christmas market. At weekends they patrol during the day as well, to contend with family parties out for a drive in the car with Grandma who are liable, if not watched, to return with Grandma sitting innocently on a pilfered Christmas tree cut down with a pruning saw.

This particular afternoon Annabel, who normally runs freely with us like a dog, was on her halter for the first part of the walk. The riding school was out and we didn't want her deciding to play with the horses, which was apt to result in people falling off in all directions. It was some time before we actually met up with the school, however, and performed our usual ritual of turning Annabel's face to a tree, as in the song about the smugglers, while the riding mistress trotted her lot past like a troop of US cavalry in the hope that they wouldn't spot her. In consequence it was some time before we could let Annabel off her halter, and Annabel was annoyed.

She loitered behind when we freed her, just to show us.

At first we didn't worry. She always caught up with us sooner or later. Then it began to get dark, and we decided perhaps we'd better round her up, otherwise, not liking to be on her own when daylight went, she might follow one of the Forestry patrol men who all this time had been passing us at regular intervals like Officers of the Watch.

Charles went back for her while I, idly swinging her halter, stood looking at the scenery. A few seconds later another of the Forestry patrol passed me and eyed me curiously. Only then did I realise how suspicious I must look — lingering there in the dusk eyeing the plantation of spruce trees, swinging in my hand what was actually a donkey halter but what, to the patrol man, must have looked very much like a rope brought to haul home a Christmas tree.

I wished him a weak good afternoon and, when he'd passed me, began to follow back behind him, hoping to meet up with Charles and Annabel and thus prove I wasn't loitering with intent. Alas, when I got to the corner where they should have been, there was no sign of either of them. I guessed at once where they were. Just beyond the corner was a deserted Forestry cottage. When people lived in it Annabel was always embarrassing us, if we didn't remember to put her on her halter first, by running through their back gate and galloping round their garden. She hadn't done it for ages, but I had no doubt that that was where she was now — and that Charles, not realising how suspicious it looked, had disappeared in there after her.

I called to him — frightening the Forestry man, who hadn't realised how close I was behind him, practically out of his wits. Placatingly I explained that my husband had gone back to look for our donkey and now they'd both disappeared. Presumably into the cottage garden, I said, and I'd better go in and look for them.

'I can see a bloke dodging about in the garden', was the reply. 'But I can't see no donkey.' I couldn't see no donkey either, until — yelling my head off to Charles and (which looked even more suspicious) getting not one peep in reply — I went round behind the cottage and there he was, too breathless to speak, chasing Annabel round and round the garden.

Eventually, after a great deal of running, we rounded her up; I pantingly enquiring of Charles why on earth he had to go in there just when there was a patrol man about who no doubt thought he was concealing a stolen tree, while Charles panted back how the Devil else was he going to get her out?

Things weren't improved meanwhile by my noticing the patrol man crouched behind the hedge and periodically peering over the top of it, undoubtedly checking on whether there really *was* a donkey in the garden with us.

It was a very docile Annabel we led on her halter for the remainder of the trip — during which, needless to say, we met no further patrol men at all. Charles said of *course* we couldn't have looked suspicious. All I knew was that I hadn't seen that particular Forestry man before. He obviously didn't know us, either, or that we owned a donkey. And for safety's sake — though we always buy it from the greengrocer anyway — I insisted that we didn't have a tree that year. I had no wish to have my Christmas festivities interrupted — undoubtedly just when the Rector was with us, having an after-church sherry on Christmas morning by the local constable and Forestry chief coming to uproot it from its pot to check on its identity.

Six: When Winter Comes

The snow started on Boxing night. We were on our way home from Charles's brother's party when the first few flakes began to fall. Congratulating ourselves that we'd got Christmas over before it started and there were still two days yet before we need think of getting through it to town, we swept down to the valley, put the car into the garage, and couldn't get it out again for a fortnight. Even after that we were only able to take advantage of a break in the weather to get it towed up to the farm at the top of the hill and use it, when practicable, from there. Six weeks in all we were snow-bound in the valley, and as a study in character it was fascinating.

There were the Hazells, for instance, who lived up the lane beyond us. This was their first winter in the valley and Jim Hazell absolutely revelled in it. Every time we looked out of the window he was trudging past dressed like a prospector in the Yukon. Up the hill to get the groceries, which he towed back down to the valley on a sledge. Up the hill to get a film — three miles it was to the nearest chemist's shop, but it was worth it, he said, to get the scenery. Up the hill to the Rose and Crown, where Father Adams encouraged him nightly by prophesying that it would be worse than ever tomorrow.

True to the pioneering spirit Jim was first, after the night when it drifted ten feet deep by the church, to climb over the top to the road. First, when it was obvious that the lane would be blocked for days, to have his car towed out by tractor across the fields. As a result he was also first to break his back axle on a frozen furrow and, pushing the car down the main road to the garage for repair, he slipped and hurt his knee. He passed our window at breakfast time like Jack London *en route* for Alaska. At lunch time he limped past in the other direction like Napoleon on the retreat from Moscow. But still he pioneered on.

A few nights later he prospected up to the Rose and Crown for his usual discussion about the weather and, while he was there, a blizzard sprang up. Half an hour later he came out into the night and headed homewards. A hundred yards along the top lane his knee gave way and he fell into the snow. The wind howled, the snow lashed like driven needles against his face, but still he got up and staggered on. He must have fallen a dozen times, he told us later, and when we asked why he hadn't come into us for help he said, in the best pioneering tradition, that he'd had to get home to Janet.

Actually he got as far as his gateway, where his wife, hearing faint cries for help above the play she was listening to on the radio, opened the door and found him practically frozen rigid on the path. She dragged him in, laid him in front of the fire to thaw him out, and bandaged his recalcitrant knee. Jolly tough stuff was Jim. Next day he was pioneering up the hill again as hard as ever and when, a while later, we heard that Janet was expecting in the autumn Father Adams said he weren't a bit surprised. Give some folk energy, the cold weather, he said.

Father Adams pioneered too, but more slowly. Mornings he trudged up the hill in his balaclava and war surplus overcoat, with an additional woollen scarf over the balaclava and, on particularly slippery days, old sacks tied for foot grip over his boots. He was helping the Council workmen clear the roads — the usual expedient of the countryman when the land itself is out of commission. When Jim complained that they hadn't got round to clearing the snowdrift by the church Father Adams said no, nor they hadn't fallen down nor broken their axles, neither, which kept Jim quiet for quite a while.

Miss Wellington was in her element. She had a thing about snow and every year she rang the Council at the sight of the first snowflake demanding that they come out and grit the lane. The Council having more vital matters to attend to, it was usually some days before they got round to us, and the next step was Miss Wellington attending to it herself up and down she bustled with her buckets of ashes, ladling them carefully with a hearth shovel not only on the part of the lane that led outwards to the main road, but backwards, down the hill to us. Why she wanted to get down to the valley — as far as he was concerned he wouldn't mind being cut off from she till Whitsun twelvemonth was Father Adams's comment when he saw her — goodness only knows. But there she was. Scraping away at the snow till the under-part shone like an ice-rink. Hacking, one bitter day, a series of steps down the side of the hill with a coal hammer, down which steps Father Adams, not knowing they were there, slid like a seal on his way home at night and wished Miss Wellington to eternity as he sat at the bottom in the snow.

Undaunted, she exhorted the rest of us to follow her example. She rang Charles one night about the drift by the church. People couldn't get through it, she explained to him earnestly. She couldn't ask the Hazells to work on it, she said. Mr Hazell had already got his car out across the fields and it wouldn't be fair to ask him. She couldn't ask the people down the lane. Their car was stuck in a snowdrift with its battery flat and quite unusable. She couldn't ask Father Adams. When Charles asked why she said she wouldn't demean herself and passed on to the upshot of her idea, which was that Charles, whom she was sure was anxious to get *his* car out, should dig his way through the snowdrift for the benefit of the community.

Apart from being ten feet deep, the snowdrift was a good fifty yards long. Charles said if he dug his way through that lot he'd be no benefit to anybody, he'd be in hospital, and after that Miss Wellington didn't demean herself by speaking to him for a week or two, either.

Meanwhile, until the snow-plough got to us, the drift was one of the local sights. People climbed it until there was a hard-packed track across it like a mountain path. We took Annabel over it one Sunday, by way of experiment, and she crossed it as sure-footedly as a goat. Single file — with Charles in front, me behind and Annabel in the middle — Annabel, we discovered, would go anywhere in the snow.

She was doing a Sarah Siddons again, of course. Annabel Crossing the Snowdrift... Annabel Doing King Wenceslas (which involved treading carefully in Charles's footsteps, head demurely bent, taking no notice whatsoever of the plaudits of passers-by)... Annabel Coming Down From The Snowdrift (a sort of Conquest of Everest in reverse in which, back to ground level but still with modestly downcast eyes, Annabel accepted apples and bullseyes from anybody who had them, allowed herself to be petted, and snorted deprecatingly to show how simple it had been)... We had all her acts in turn, but at least she got some exercise.

So — at times rather more than we expected — did we.

There was the day, for instance, when, exhilarated by the way she'd gone over the church drift, we decided to bring her back via another. Through the drift on this occasion, for it was in a lane unused by anyone, but it was only about two feet deep and as we forged our way through the virgin snow — Annabel behind us this time, while we broke the trail ahead of her —

we felt like Yukon prospectors ourselves. Unfortunately it got deeper as we went on. Soon we were pushing through it more than waist-deep, Annabel obediently behind us — until, in a particularly stubborn spot, I happened to look back to see her standing with her head laid resignedly on the snowdrift, her eyes closed, and her nose a peculiar indigo blue.

We'd read that a donkey in a tight corner can make up its mind to die and do so, but this was the first time we'd experienced it ourselves. By the colour of her nose Annabel had decided to die pretty fast, too. We scooped the snow panic-strickenly away from her with our hands, pivoted her on her hind legs and carried her, stiff as a ramrod, back to open country as fast as we could stagger. She recovered as quickly as she'd wilted, of course. Ten yards out from the drift her nose was back to normal and she was capering happily in the snow trying to bite our ankles. Only we, having, in our extremity, lifted a small fat donkey who for years we hadn't even been able to push, were feeling the worse for wear. Didn't run about and enjoy ourselves very much, did we? enquired Annabel disappointedly when we refused to play.

The next time we took her out I was the casualty. She got demonstrably bored tramping to and fro like a Holloway trusty along the twelve-foot path from her house to the hurdle gate, which was all we'd been able to clear for her in the two feet of snow that covered her paddock, and when we appeared with her halter it was always a cause for exuberance. When, therefore, I put my cheek against hers, enquired tenderly whether she was going out, and Annabel upped with her head to indicate less of the soft stuff, open the gate and get going Pronto, it was my own fault entirely. It didn't alter the fact that she'd nearly broken my nose, though. Clutching it, my eyes filled with tears, I staggered in painful circles outside her gate.

Blood started dripping on to the snow, too — a sight at which I felt even sorrier for myself.

Charles, starting to comfort me, at that moment spotted people coming down the hill. 'Shh — they'll hear you', he said — Charles being the typical British type who believes in keeping a stiff upper lip in front of strangers. Still holding my nose, groaning that it was broken and nobody cared, I reeled into Annabel's house and sat sadly in the straw till the people had gone, ruminating on the debit side of keeping a donkey.

I had my revenge sooner than I expected. After the people had gone I came out of the donkey house, Charles having assured me that my nose was still in one piece; Annabel tugged at my duffle coat to show that it had all been in fun; and we set out belatedly on our walk. Through the Valley; up the Slagger's Path to the village, along which the old-time miners used to carry the lead; back past the caravan where the singer lives, who to Father Adams's disgust grows geraniums in his wheelbarrow in the summer and Wur, Father Adams comments loudly every time he passes, do the tomfool put his weeds?

We were passing the caravan ourselves, Annabel doing her swaying pack-donkey walk in case there was anybody inside to see her, when she picked up a cigarette packet. Vastly pleased that we laughed at her, she trudged on, carrying the packet in her mouth like a dog with a bone, till I said I wished somebody could see her; nobody'd ever believe she'd do that sort of thing just by our telling them. At that moment two people did come into view, climbing up the hill towards us, whereupon Annabel drew the packet inside her mouth — still, however, leaving enough outside to show that it was a cigarette packet — and proceeded to eat it.

She would, I said with feeling. Carry it like a circus act for ten minutes and the moment we passed anybody you bet she'd eat it, just to show people how hungry she was and how we starved her.

There was no answer from Charles. Looking around from my position on Annabel's right I discovered that, suddenly, there was no Charles, either. Peering over Annabel's broad brown back I saw him kneeling, redfaced, on her other side. When I asked what he was doing he staggered to his feet and began limping in circles himself. Slipped on the ice, he informed me. Broken his kneecap (which he hadn't, actually; fortunately it was only bruised). Couldn't I do something, he demanded, continuing to reel in circles and at the same time hold his knee, which was quite a feat on the slippery ice. I was laughing so much I nearly fell down myself. Not to make a *fuss*, I said hysterically. Remember what he'd told *me*. People might *hear*, and what on earth would they think?

Charles had to laugh himself at that, and Annabel, chewing placidly away at her cigarette packet, glanced curiously at us over her shoulder. Couple of nut cases was her verdict.

Robertson seconded that before the winter was out. By this time he had taken to sleeping in the garage. Annabel was all *right*, he explained to us in his reedy little voice the first time we found him there, but she would walk in and out over the snow and it made the straw all damp to sleep on, whereas in the garage there was nice dry hay. Just the thing for a cat like him in weather like this, he wheedled, weaving ingratiatingly round our legs. Helped keep the mice away, he proffered as an additional inducement, seeing that we were obviously wavering. So now he slept in the garage, had his milk in there to make sure he got it himself instead of a donkey who was already overweight, and though Annabel nudged him pettishly when he joined her in the mornings by way of reproach for his absence, he merely brushed his bushy tail against her nose, assured her that he'd been on important business where donkeys couldn't go, and settled down to breakfast.

Solomon's activities at this time being given over to bird watching in the yard outside the kitchen, while Sheba, complaining that it made her feet cold, rarely went outside at all, Robertson now took to accompanying Charles most possessively from garage to donkey-house, and from donkey-house back to garage. Probably for the first time in years he had a feeling of belonging, which was undoubtedly how the trouble arose.

The Hazells went to London for a weekend, asking us to stoke their Aga and feed their ginger cat, Rufus, while they were away. The first night we went up Rufus was ready and waiting, one eye on the Aga and the other on the refrigerator. The next morning he was there too, bawling vociferously for us to get cracking with the tin-opener, *that* was the tin he fancied today. That night he was missing, however, and it was only after we'd been there quite a few minutes, stoking the Aga and refilling the fuel hod, that I spotted him watching us through the window.

He was sitting out on the lawn, at the edge of the light patch cast by the kitchen window. Perhaps he was suddenly nervous of us, we thought. Resentful maybe of the fact that there were strangers in his house. He had his own way in, but, wishing to see him eat before we left, we went to the door and called him. He came to the threshold but would come no further, so Charles picked him up. His hand raked from stem to stern, Charles hastily put him down again. *This* was the way to carry a strange cat, I said, grasping him by the scruff of his neck, my other hand taking the weight of his feet, and scuttling speedily in to deposit him in the hall. Rufus bolted immediately through the lounge door, which was open, and sat just inside it, on the edge of the divan. There he stayed in the semi-darkness while we clattered his food-dishes, rattled the tin-opener and made enticing noises from the kitchen. Finally we gave it up, wished him goodnight as we passed, and unlatched the front door. What made me go back and take a closer look at him in the torchlight I don't know — but when I did, it wasn't Rufus at all. It was Robertson.

He'd *said* he didn't want to go in, he protested as I hurried him out. He didn't *like* being in houses, anyway, he said as we found the real Rufus hiding behind the coalbunker, carried him in and gave him his supper at last.

Only *came* to go walks with Charles, wailed Robertson plaintively from the garden.

Waving the empty tin under his nose we enticed him home so he wouldn't disturb Rufus, locked him in the garage for the night with some supper of his own, and went back to our fireside. Solomon sniffed suspiciously at us for the rest of the night like Sherlock Holmes, saying we'd been with other cats. Sheba went and sat in the hall as the nearest thing she could think of to leaving home without getting her feet cold. Honestly, we couldn't win!

Seven: And Spring is Far Behind

That was the winter we became so friendly with the blackbird. He'd been with us for years; chivvying us for food from the corner of the woodshed roof in the mornings; baiting Solomon, when he felt in a merry mood, by fluttering low across the lawn with Fatso leaping like a trout in pursuit; turning ragged as a scarecrow every summer because he was by no means young and raising families at the rate he raised them certainly took it out of a bird.

This particular winter, however, he took to actually coming into the kitchen when he wanted food, walking flat-footedly through the door at ground level like a clockwork penguin on a pavement in Oxford Street.

Sheba, who never missed anything, promptly took to sitting behind the door waiting for him. Solomon — without the faintest idea of what they were in ambush for but he always joined Sheba if he saw her doing anything interesting — took to sitting hopefully alongside her. A situation that gave us a dozen fits a day until we discovered that the blackbird was a lot wiser than he looked. Peer through the partly open door, which had to be kept ajar even in the coldest weather otherwise Solomon used it as a Wailing Wall, battering frantically at it howling to be let out, he couldn't breathe, claustrophobia was setting in — and there, while two Siamese waited expectantly on one side, the blackbird, with his head cocked, stood listening intently on the other. Waiting till they went away before he pattered familiarly in, and he never made a mistake.

He made a mistake in another direction, however. He took to staying up late to see us. If we got home at dusk on a winter's evening, there, long after the other birds had gone to roost, a solitary little black figure sat waiting on the coalhouse roof, chattering, presumably to tell us all the day's doings, as we came down the path.

One night we came home well after dark, trudging down the hill from the farm through the snow, and while Charles opened up the garage to get Annabel's hay, I went on into the cottage, switching on the porch and hall lights as I did so. There was no sign of the blackbird. At that time of night we wouldn't have expected him. I was halfway through the hall when I heard a noise as of a bird crashing against the window and rushed outside again. There was no sign of anything. No bird lying stunned in the snow. No bird anywhere in the garden. Charles said he wouldn't be so stupid, anyway, as to be trying to contact us at that time of night. But — roused presumably by my switching on the porch light — he must have been. The next morning, when we opened the kitchen door, he was squatting on the coalhouse roof with his legs folded under him. Damaged by the bang on the window, and now what were we to do?

He wouldn't let us near enough to catch him, and we were obviously only frightening him by our attempts, so we did the best we could by throwing a large sheet of cardboard on to the lawn where it would catch the sun. Throwing it, because that way it landed like a raft on a three-foot depth of untrammelled snow which even the most determined pair of Siamese were unlikely to cross unless they could borrow a sledge.

We tossed bread and bacon rind on to the cardboard and the blackbird got the idea at once. There he fed, and sat safe from ambush on the dry cardboard, while the faint March sun did its work. He stayed there, apart from exercise flights, for days. We propped the coalhouse door open and hoped he used that for shelter by night. Just in case he slept in the porch instead we bolted the front door at dusk, took the lamp bulbs out of the porch and hall lights so we wouldn't switch on by accident and disturb him, and in consequence had to grope for the hall table every time the telephone rang and Charles tripped upstairs twice.

It was worth it in the end. The blackbird's legs had been bruised, probably numbed by the cold, but not broken.

First one and then the other returned to normal. The moment the first one was functioning he flew down and stood on it in the kitchen doorway to show us, chittering mockingly at the cats whom this manoeuvre had left sitting on the hall window-sill planning, from the expressions on their faces, how they could best throw a breeches buoy across the lawn and get out to the cardboard that way.

They'd have been a lot more useful if they'd taken a course in mining. Apart from the drifts the snow was going rapidly now, and as it melted from the big top lawn we discovered that another inhabitant of the great outdoors, hearing no doubt that we were fond of animals, had decided to live with us. We now had a resident mole.

Dozens of them, it seemed, watching the hillocks rear up like mountain ranges where once there was flat green lawn, but Father Adams said 'twere only one and offered to set a trap. Charles said we couldn't do a thing like that and it was a marvellous chance to study it. I didn't want it trapped either, but I drew the line at studying it on our front lawn. The day Charles came in and said if I went out quietly I could actually *see* it — it had looked at him out of a hole, he said, and how many people could say they'd seen *that* in their garden? I enquired which hillock he'd seen it in, went outside, and jumped. Not on the hillock itself I had no wish to harm the mole. I just thought a few local tremors might move it off.

It worked. Some people going along the lane looked at me a bit peculiarly when they saw me doing what appeared to be a war-dance round a molehill, but it worked. We had no more mole heaps on that lawn. One or two appeared rather tentatively on the lower lawn, but when I jumped on that, those stopped too.

Unfortunately the mole then went berserk and submerged under the paving-stones that Charles was laying in the yard, its progress marked by long thin lines of earth rising, like the smoke from an excursion train, between the cracks. Rather on my conscience that was, imagining him coming up for air to be repeatedly met by paving-stones, and it was a great relief when his trail turned once more towards the lower lawn … no jumping on it this time; we didn't want him under those paving-stones again … across it, and finally OUT. Under the wall and across into the woods, where presumably he lives to this day telling of his adventures in the earthquake country.

The winter — the worst winter we'd had for years — was passing now, but two relics of it remained with us as inexorably as the Laws of the Medes and Persians. Annabel's addiction to a hot drink at bedtime and the cats' decision to sleep downstairs. Annabel's discovery of hot drinks had come about not as a result of our pampering her, but of our trying to ensure that she got a drink at all. On principle she wouldn't drink when we first took her bucket out. Didn't want it. Didn't *like* water anyway, she would snort when we offered it to her. By the time she did feel like it the bucket was invariably frozen, so we started pouring a kettleful of hot water in before we carried it up in the hope of it staying liquid longer. Annabel, intrigued by the steam, immediately investigated it. The warmth to her nose must have been wonderful … even more so to her stomach, when it got down on all that hay…

She drank it as if it were nectar, with long sucking noises and a smack of her lips at the end. We, knowing how we liked our own hot drinks, took to giving it to her regularly, and as a result, long after the frost had gone and the lighter nights were coming we were still chugging up in the evenings with a steaming bucket which, if we saw anybody coming, we hid surreptitiously in the greenhouse. We had no wish to reveal to people that if we now tried to make her go to bed without a hot drink, our donkey bawled the place down.

We were in a similar position with the cats. Ever since they were born they had, unless we had visitors, slept next door to us in the spare room. There, if they fought in the night or fell out of bed or decided that they didn't feel well, we could hear them at once and go to the rescue. There was also the advantage of their being unable to damage the furniture in there, the only upholstered item being the armchair in which they slept, whose covering and Hessian under-part they had demolished long ago, as kittens.

It was so cold that winter, however, that even with two hot-water bottles they had us up at two in the morning protesting that their ears were falling off, please to let them into bed with us. We got no sleep if we did. Solomon, being my cat, insisted on cuddling cheek to cheek with me. If Sheba showed signs of wanting to get in on my side he got closer still and lay possessively on my face. If she did come in he bit her on the leg, whereupon Sheba spat like a squib and went and sat forlornly at the bottom. She wouldn't sleep on Charles's side. Charles, she said, fidgeted. She either sat despondently on my feet and got cold, or came back and we had a repeat performance with Solomon. Solomon, if he finally did relent and let her in, in any case snored and twitched his paws like a tic-tac man the moment he fell asleep. So in the end we fixed them up in the sitting-room.

Bottles and blankets in the big armchair in front of the fire. The fire made up so the room wouldn't get cold during the night. Food, water-bowl and earth-boxes conveniently lined up so that they had the equivalent of a luxury self-contained flat. Thereafter we went to bed leaving two little cats sitting happily on the hearthrug in the firelight in a manner that reminded us of a Christmas card. A picture, alas, that resolved itself, the moment we ourselves were in bed, into the sound of claws being stropped down below us in celebration on the chair covers; the sound of a Siamese Grand National by firelight over the furniture (in friendship this time, as we could tell from the change of direction as Solomon chasing Sheba gave way, to his intense delight, to Sheba chasing Solomon); and the reply as we shouted and banged on the floor in protest, from a basso profundo Seal-point voice assuring us that everything was all right down *there*. He and Sheba were enjoying themselves.

They enjoyed themselves to the extent that, within days, they were trying to send *us* to bed. Come eleven o'clock and Solomon would start rubbing against Charles's foot. Sheba would practise long-jumps from chair to chair. Solomon, when all else failed, would sit on the back of the armchair in which they slept and wail, with his eyes fixed on the door through which we must go to fill their hot-water bottles and clean our teeth, that it was Late ... he was getting Circles under his eyes from staying up... Sheba had circles too, he would shout, Sheba being Charles's cat and Solomon thought that might speed him up a bit...

There was no question of moving them back upstairs when the winter ended. They were down there for good.

Things were progressing everywhere now. Mrs Adams had taken down the maroon plush curtains and replaced them with spring-like white muslin. Father Adams was pursuing the traditional country pastime of having a row with his neighbour over their boundary. Miss Wellington was painting her garden gnomes — a task which, as there were eight of them plus an assortment of spotted toadstools, ensured that she was on the other side of the wall, brushing away with an air of intense absorption, every time the row over the boundary disturbed the desert air. And there was tension at the Rose and Crown.

There usually was. From who pulled the bells wrong on Sunday to the way some hapless newcomer was growing his potatoes, they were always in a state over something. This time, however, it appeared that disaster had really struck.

A Mr Carey had bought a cottage in the lane adjoining the side entrance to the pub. He'd decided to build a garage at the side of the cottage and to alter his existing gate and run-in, which was right outside his front door, to an entrance further along that would also serve the garage. While he was walling up the old entrance he'd further decided to front it with what he considered to be an improvement — a steep bank of earth, in line with the other grass verges along the lane, planted with heather roots that he'd brought back from his walks.

Unfortunately other people didn't see it like that. The old way in, being right opposite the pub's side entrance, had been the one place in the whole lane where cars could squeeze past while the brewery lorry was unloading. Every time there was a beer delivery now there was a queue of car owners honking agitatedly to pass. The brewery driver got bad-tempered having to keep breaking off to move the lorry. Father Adams said it didn't do the beer no good, being rolled in in all that hurry. Mr Carey — a nondrinker himself and entirely unmoved by such sentiments — said why didn't they unload the lorry at the front door of the pub … a suggestion, entirely feasible, which was rejected out of hand on the grounds that the lorry had always been unloaded at the side door and who was he to alter things?

The matter had been referred urgently to the Parish Council. Unfortunately they met only every two months. Meanwhile there was a weekly traffic block at Carey's cottage, a nightly indignation meeting at the Rose and Crown, and considerable speculation as to whether the heather, planted so doggedly by Mr Carey, would grow.

General opinion was that it wouldn't. It grew in the peat on top of the moors, but hereabouts the soil was limestone. Actually it did. In bringing the heather down from the moors Mr Carey had thoughtfully brought the soil to go with it. And there, for the moment, the matter rested.

Things were much more peaceful with us. For one thing Solomon appeared to have made friends with Robertson. I nearly dropped the first time I saw them, Robertson ensconced inscrutably on a hay-bale in the garage and Solomon, on his first post-thaw inspection trip, sitting on the ground in front of him. There was a silence that I expected to be broken at any moment by Solomon hurtling flat-eared into the attack. Then I realised it was a silence not so much of an eve of battle as of a chess-match. Robertson regarded the driveway. Solomon studied the sand-heap. There they sat, if a trifle embarrassedly, like a couple of members of Boodles.

It was some time before Sheba joined them, but eventually she did and now the three of them sat in silence in the garage apparently practising mental telepathy. They weren't practising that, though, the evening we saw them by the woodshed. We'd been off for a week by the sea — Annabel going up to the farm, Solomon and Sheba to the Siamese hotel at Halstock, and the Hazells, in our absence, feeding Robertson. Halfway through the week he'd vanished, they reported when we came back, and they couldn't find him anywhere. We thought he'd probably traced Annabel to the farm and sure enough, the day after we fetched Annabel home, Robertson himself reappeared, stalking grandly along the path towards her stable.

Later that night I noticed, looking through the kitchen doorway, that Solomon and Sheba were in the yard, sitting in front of the woodshed and studying the base of it with expressions of rapt concentration. 'They've got Robertson down a mouse-hole,' I jokingly said to Charles, 'and they're not going to let him come out.' I was nearer the truth than I knew. A while later I looked out of the hall window on the principle, well-known to Siamese owners, that if they're quiet they're up to something — and there, beyond them, where I hadn't been able to see him from the kitchen, was Robertson. Sniffing at one of the support posts while our two gazed superiorly on.

A little later Robertson had gone, but our own two were still sitting importantly by the woodshed. I went out at that to see what Robertson had been sniffing at — and there, down the woodwork, was a long damp streak. Solomon, it seemed, had sprayed. A good big spray that he'd been saving up for a week. He'd then sat down with Sheba with an air of Beat That One If You Can while Robertson inspected it — and, to their intense satisfaction, he'd had to admit that he couldn't.

Eight: Music Hath Charms

Had things continued like that, with Robertson content to sit outcast-fashion in the yard, to acknowledge Solomon as local spraying champion and to look suitably humble whenever our two met up with him, they might in time have become used to him and allowed him into the cottage.

Might is a nebulous word, of course. They might equally have done what they did years before when we tried to introduce the kitten Samson. Fight him, ourselves and each other till the place resembled the United Nations.

As it was, Robertson jumped the gun one day and appeared in person in our kitchen. Without being asked, commented Sheba, who was the first to spot him and drew our attention to it by craning her neck incredulously through the doorway from the sitting-room. Just going to eat Our Food! roared Solomon — which Robertson probably was, but only because it happened to be there, like the fruits of the Indies, *en route* on his voyage of discovery...

Robertson went through the door like a niblick shot with Solomon behind him. Any time Solomon saw Robertson after that he chased him indignantly from the garden. That, hard though it was on Robertson, was logical. It was Solomon's garden; Robertson *was* supposed to live with Annabel; and though I felt a pang at times when I saw his stocky ginger figure valiantly accompanying Charles around the orchard or sitting with him while he dug in the vegetable garden, which was the nearest Robertson could come now to his desire to belong to somebody, at least he got regular meals and we petted him surreptitiously in the garage.

He was sitting by the bean row one day, busily belonging to Charles, when some people came past with a dog. The dog, a big brown cross-bred, stopped in the gateway and growled at Robertson. Only in passing, because Robertson was a cat, but Robertson didn't see it like that. He saw it that Solomon stopped him from being with Charles in the cottage; now this dog was threatening to stop him from being with Charles among the beans... At that point something snapped. He stood up, bushed his tail, and growled back. The dog fled. Robertson, like a boy who has just discovered he can fight a bully, flew after him. The snag being that the next time he saw Solomon, he flew at *him*.

'Take that ... and that ... and THAT', he spat, and Solomon, caught unawares, was badly beaten. Thereafter it was Solomon versus Butch all over again. Solomon kept going out to look for Robertson. Robertson kept coming down to look for Solomon. He was worse than Butch, however, in that his idea was obviously to drive Solomon away from the cottage so that he could live with us himself. The blue one, too, he apparently decided, with the result that he leapt from the undergrowth one day when Sheba and I were in the garden — Sheba, who had never said boo to him in her life ... and attacked her before my very eyes until, recovering from my surprise, I shouted and drove him off.

Thereafter I was officially his enemy. Behind the scenes I still prepared his food — there was nobody else to feed him and we couldn't let him starve. But Charles took it up to him. Charles talked to him and allowed Robertson to accompany him round the orchard. Any time I saw him, I chased him back to the paddock. I hated doing it, but it was the only way. He had Charles as his friend, lived with Annabel, had good meals, but knew that if he set one paw in the garden I'd be after him.

It was no worse, in principle, than a cat living in one house but being afraid to venture next door because of the dog — and that way, we thought, we could look after him yet keep our own two safe from attack.

It worked for a while. Robertson loved Charles, looked daggers at me when he saw me, but kept well to his side of the fence. When he went for a ramble he skirted our garden now, instead of coming through it. Our two, for their part, took to the tiles for safety — Sheba sitting on the coalhouse under the lilac, which was in any case a favourite perch of hers, and Solomon spending most of his time on the woodshed. It was higher, the woodshed roof, and Solomon, though officially up there looking for Robertson, obviously felt safer at an altitude.

He wasn't, though. Stumping with the resentfulness of the underprivileged past the cottage one day, Robertson spotted Solomon in his eyrie, presumably worked out that he could get at him up there without setting foot in the forbidden territory of our garden (the only reason I can think of for the fact that his approach from then on was always from an outside wall at roof level, and never by any chance through the yard) and climbed metaphorically in with his cosh.

Thereafter I dreaded ten o'clock in the morning. Around that time Robertson came by on the war-path. If Solomon was on the woodshed he got up and attacked him. If Sheba was on the coalhouse, he got up and attacked her. Keep vigilance as I might, the moment my back was turned he was up there fighting one of them.

Sheba, rolling comet-fashion as in her battle with Butch, was off the roof and indoors within seconds. Solomon, however, apart from his determination to fight like a man, couldn't roll off the woodshed. It was too high to get off in a hurry. He had to stay there till I went to his aid. Becoming, for some reason we couldn't understand, less and less able to drive Robertson off until the day came — or so we imagined must have happened — when Robertson pushed Solomon off the roof.

We rushed out to find him limping slowly through the yard while Robertson made off up the lane. He limped, he wouldn't eat … he was Tired, he said. All he wanted was to lie down and rest. We got the Vet at once; this time not without cause. He hadn't fallen off the roof, said Mr Harler — or if he had, it hadn't done him any harm. What Solomon had was a virus infection. A high temperature, a resultant lethargy which was why he hadn't felt like fighting. When I asked but why was he limping if he hadn't fallen off the roof, Mr Harler said 'You'd limp too, if your legs were aching', and called him his poor little man.

He gave him aureomycin. Afterwards, sick at heart to think of him being attacked while he was ill, by a cat whom we'd encouraged, perhaps from whom he'd actually caught the infection while they were fighting, we watched him limp listlessly up behind the cottage into the long grass.

'Let him rest for a while', the Vet had said after the injection. And so, working in the garden to guard him, watching perpetually for Robertson, we did. Never giving a thought to the heat of the sun except that the warmth would do him good, until, going up to see how he was an hour later, I found him suffering from heat-stroke.

It was obvious enough. His legs were aching, the injection had made him sleepy, the strength of the sun had intensified the effect until he was too numb to move even if he'd wanted to. So obvious that we hadn't even thought of it.

Anguishedly I picked him up — limp, his head drooping over my arm, dribbling helplessly at the mouth — and rushed indoors with him to Charles. We laid him on our bed, which was the coolest place we could think of, and pulled the curtains. So many pictures went through my mind while we watched and waited. Solomon as a kitten, running races up and down this very bed. Solomon going walks with us, galloping exuberantly on his long black legs to catch us when we ran. Solomon, so nervous for all his airs of bravado, coming to me when he was frightened, looking into my eyes for reassurance when he was in the hands of the Vet, trusting me with every inch of his small seal-point soul — and I had let him down.

He wasn't our little black clown for nothing, however. Even as I gulped back my tears — Solomon was scared of crying; he always hid under the table when I wept — Sheba came into the room. On to the bed she got. Sniffed Solomon expertly. Informed us in her cracked soprano voice that there wasn't much wrong with *him*, and went to sit, unconcernedly washing herself, in the window behind the curtains.

She was right. Half an hour later he was sitting up drinking rabbit broth. That night he was eating rabbit itself. Within two days, so quickly did the aureomycin work, he was back to normal. Eating like a horse. Going, every time he thought of it, right up to the paddock to challenge Robertson (only I went right up after him and brought him back before he got the chance). Robertson, sensing his disgrace, stayed strictly up with Annabel. In order to divert Solomon's mind from Robertson we took him and Sheba for walks. Which was how we came to buy a piano.

We took them up across the hills one night — Charles carrying Sheba, who was otherwise apt to say her feet hurt and turn back halfway, while Solomon ambled behind. Rounding a corner, we suddenly came upon a young man sitting in a hedge with a tape-recorder. Recording birdsong, we presumed; we couldn't think what he was doing there otherwise. Not wanting to disturb him, we put Sheba down with Solomon and turned quietly back along the track.

Normally this was the signal for the pair of them to follow back behind us, bounding exuberantly through the grass and stopping at intervals to play their favourite game of boys and girls, which consisted of Solomon sitting on Sheba and biting her neck and which, for some reason best known to themselves, they only did on the return half of walks.

This time, however, there was silence. No sign of anybody. Until we went back along the track once more and there round the corner sat the pair of them, side by side in front of the bird-watcher. There was no need for speech. The angle of Sheba's ears enquired what he was doing. The angle of Solomon's expressed intense interest in the recorder itself. Silently we picked them up and slung them over our shoulders. Silently, if somewhat bewilderedly, the birdwatcher acknowledged our mimed apology...

It was useless, of course. Hanging over our shoulders as we tiptoed down the track, they started to shout back at him. Sheba first, as she always did to departing strangers, Solomon joining in from sheer enthusiasm. There went *that* recording, I said resignedly. While Charles, his mind on the recorder itself, said 'When are we going to get our piano?'

He'd been wanting one for ages. He was fond of music. If we had a piano, he commented at frequent intervals, I could accompany him while he played the violin, and he'd learn the piano himself so he could compose.

Neither of us had played at all for a considerable number of years. It was, as I pointed out, going to cause something of a sensation in the Valley when we started *our* duets. Charles practising beginners' pieces on a piano would hardly go unnoticed, either. Couldn't he compose on a violin? I enquired hopefully.

Apparently he couldn't. He needed a piano. Having settled that, the project stayed in the background for months and might never have materialised at all but for Charles seeing the tape-recorder turning seductively in the hedge.

That — and the visions it no doubt aroused of composing, recording, and the tapes being sent to London to be played by an ecstatic Barbirolli — revived his interest, and within a fortnight we had our piano. A modern miniature. And the piano men had gone, and I was in the study trying it out.

My one real doubt about having it had been how Solomon would react. He was a tremendously nervous cat. The staccato tap of a typewriter, for instance, affected him so that he leapt like a startled fawn at the slightest sound for hours after either of us had used it. We'd long ago had to buy a silent model before we started leaping too. So we'd decided to get him used to the piano gradually. Shut him downstairs to begin with, where he could only hear it at a distance, and then let him come up to the study in his own good time, exploring by himself.

In the excitement I forgot that, of course. I'd locked Solomon and Sheba in our bedroom while the piano was delivered. Let them out afterwards, when they'd immediately rushed down to see what they'd missed. And I'd started, hesitantly, to play.

After all those years of not touching a piano it probably was pretty awful — but not, I feel sure, as excruciating as I was given to understand when I glanced up a few minutes later to see the two of them sitting side by side in the doorway looking at me. There was no sign of nervousness on Solomon's face. Only complete incredulity. What on earth did I think I was doing? His expression demanded. Frightening off the bogy-men? Sheba enquired, while two pairs of ears tilted speculatively towards the piano.

After that I had only to touch the keys and, even if they hadn't been seen for hours, they appeared as if I were the Pied Piper of Hamelin. It wasn't so much the music. It was warm just then, and when I played I opened the window that looked out on to the hall roof for air. The attraction was to get up into the wide, tiled window-sill and march in and out over the roof with raised tails, as if they were playing at bands. I reckoned they were doing it to draw people's attention to the fact that we now possessed a piano. Charles said they were making sure nobody thought it was them making all that noise. Whichever it was, the fact remained that the sun shone straight through that window on to the music rack; that when I played it was with the shadows of a pair of Siamese tails passing continuously across the music like a frieze of travelling bulrushes; and that when from time to time the voice of Father Adams saying 'Cor!' floated up from the lane as I struck a particularly distracted chord, it was hardly to be wondered at.

There are so many things one can do with a piano. When they came finally in from the roof, for instance, they jumped heavily, one by one, on to my back *en route* to the floor. That laid me practically flat on the keyboard for a start. Occasionally, inspired by a particularly noisy piece of music, they staged a wrestling match on the stairs. Galvanised on one occasion by the sound of louder screams than usual, I looked up to see Sheba crawling through the doorway on her stomach while Solomon held her by the scruff of the neck. This do for Rigoletto? they enquired hopefully.

One night Solomon rushed excitedly upstairs in the middle of my practising and bit me on the leg. Only in fun, of course.

Apparently he'd decided I was playing the piano as a joke, so he was playing one on me. He beamed all over his triangular black face when I yelled and leapt from the chair.

Another night Sheba decided to sit on top of the door to watch me — a favourite place of hers — and, just as I got to the difficult bit, she fell off. Half a page of Chopin followed by a scream and the sound of somebody apparently being thrown from top to bottom of the stairs — that was the order of the day with my piano practice.

Charles had even less success. He'd intended to learn from the Rector's wife, who'd had quite a few pupils in the village, but she and her husband had moved to another parish. There wasn't a teacher now within miles. While he waited for one to turn up — if not, said Charles, he'd buy a Tutor when he had time and teach himself; the important thing was to have the piano — he got out his violin. That was in a pretty parlous state, too; the strings long since disintegrated, the bow a wreck, the bridge lying forlornly on its side in the case. Charles went specially to town to renew everything and one night stood happily in the sitting-room, violin assembled, ready to begin.

'Now!' he said with confidence, raising his bow.

I should have anticipated it, of course. Charles, with practice, is an extremely good violinist. A violin is a tricky thing, however, and after a lapse of years anyone's notes are liable to be off.

Charles's were so off that Solomon, who'd been sleeping peacefully on the hearthrug, was up and in siege position at the top of the stairs before the echo of the first one had died away. He wore his Loch Ness Monster expression and, as Charles drew his next, more tentative, bow across the strings, retired beneath the bed. Somebody was murdering somebody in his opinion, and he didn't want to be included.

It was obviously a choice between his nerves and the violin, and when it got to the stage where he went and sat on the landing if I so much as moved the violin case to dust it, Solomon, as usual, won.

The violin went back into the cupboard. Charles bought himself a piano tutor. He put it aside for the moment, being busy with other things — but the day would come, he informed Solomon darkly. Solomon regarded him innocently. He liked *pianos*, he assured him.

Nine: Getting Things Moving

Charles wasn't the only one affected by the Rector's departure. Father Adams had been cutting the Rectory lawn for years and when the new man, the Reverend Morgan, moved in bringing with him a motor mower and the announcement that he liked using it himself, for exercise, our neighbour was very put out indeed.

He pretended not to recognise Mr Morgan when they met. Ours being a quiet village, there were times when the only figures visible in the entire place were the stocky, betrilbied outline of Father Adams crossing the Green to the Rose and Crown and the tall thin black one of the Rector emerging on some errand from the Rectory, but still Father Adams affected not to see him.

He sentimentalised about his predecessor over his nightly pint until Mr Holcombe, whose most errant sheep Father Adams had ever been, would never have recognised himself. He passed the Rectory gate as though even to glance at it would turn him immediately to a pillar of salt. It was a situation ripe for Siamese exploitation and at an opportune moment Father Adams's own Siamese, Mimi, exploited it.

We didn't see much of Mimi these days. She, and the picture painted of her incredible attributes by Father Adams, had been responsible for our going in for Siamese in the first place, but by the time Solomon and Sheba had grown up she'd given up coming down to us. Our two had told her on too many occasions what would happen if she did. She never normally went near the Rectory either, being content — being a lady, and on her own, which has a more sobering effect when cats grow older than keeping them in pairs — to sit on her own home gatepost and study the passers-by.

There she was now, however, on the Rectory wall as large as life, bawling to Father Adams to see where she was, and he, sweating frantically with the embarrassment of it, trying to get her down. She wouldn't jump on his shoulder. She liked it up there, she said. She wasn't interested in a wiggled twig. Remember where she was, she intimated with dignity. She sat there playing the part of the Squire's lady, as the Squire's lady might play it if she held her At Homes on top of the Rectory wall. Father Adams got exasperated and eventually threw his hat at her to try to move her. Mimi stopped playing at visiting and was down, across the Green and sitting on her own home gatepost with the speed of a Derby winner. Which was why the hat, instead of bouncing off her, went over the wall; Father Adams wouldn't go in and ask for it; and for the first time in living memory … at least for fifty years, we gathered from the discussion that went on about it afterwards … he stumped self-consciously home through the village, hatless.

He might as well have come through it trouserless. Faces appeared at the windows as he passed. Somebody asked him if 'twere cold up top. Miss Wellington rose slowly from the gnome she was painting, stared incredulously after him and, paintbrush in hand, disappeared immediately through the next-door gate to spread the news.

Actually it was a blessing in disguise. The hat (nobody could have mistaken that battered coal-scuttle effect as anybody but Father Adams's even if it had been found on the railings of Buckingham Palace) appeared, tilted at a rakish angle, on the Adams's front gatepost an hour later. The Rector grinned so knowingly at Father Adams next time they met that Father Adams couldn't help grinning back. The next we heard, Mr

Morgan had decided that he couldn't, after all, manage all that grass by himself and the familiar outline of Father Adams was once more seen progressing importantly over the Rectory lawn on Saturday afternoons — this time, to his intense satisfaction, behind a large and exceedingly noisy motor mower. Them cats certainly got things moving, he remarked, leaning reflectively on our gate one night.

So, if it came to that, did donkeys. We'd recently been given permission to graze Annabel on the adjoining Forestry Commission land, the only stipulation being that we should tether her to prevent her eating the trees. Surrounded by all the lush green grass that was a welcome change from her own moth-eaten paddock, Annabel wasn't the slightest bit interested in the trees, but we tethered her all the same. It prevented her from chasing horse-riders as they rode up the Forestry tracks.

It also, since one can't have everything in this world, presented us with an entirely new set of problems. Tether her to a tree and within minutes, having walked round it determinedly in circles, she'd be bound to it like Joan of Arc, bawling for help. Tether her on what appeared to be open land and in no time she'd be roped, head down and unable to move, round an ant-hill. Tether her, as we did once, on a piece flat as a billiard table with her rope tied to a last-war bayonet left behind by the previous owner of the cottage — she couldn't wind her rope round that, said Charles, and it made a jolly good portable anchor … the next thing we knew, a posse of round-eyed children were coming in to report that Annabel had a sword, and when we scurried out, sure enough there was Annabel running round in the lane with the bayonet clanking behind her.

We dared not try that one again. We went back to tethering her to trees. It meant we had to keep going out to unwind her, but it was safer. Until, that was, we tethered her to a felled Scots pine, high on the Valley skyline, in the belief that she couldn't move that one in a hundred years. Five minutes later Annabel, complete with pine tree to which she was still attached, was down in the Valley bottom. Right by our back gate, where our immediate problem was to get the tree up again double quick, before the Forestry people thought we were stealing it.

It was sooner said than done. At that point the hillside was practically perpendicular. The tree weighed at least a ton. Sweatingly we tugged and strained — with Annabel tied to the front end ostensibly helping us but a fat lot of help that donkey gave, if I knew anything about it. At last we got it up. It would have been better if we'd untied Annabel from it before we sat down to rest, of course, but one can't think of everything. In any case we were too worn out. So we sat there panting, with the sweat dripping off our brows, Annabel said that was fun, wasn't it, and started trotting down the hill again log and all. We got up and chased her...

It wasn't my day that day. I had got past the log and was close behind her when Annabel swerved and the rope tripped me up. While I was sitting there swearing soundly the log, which I had forgotten, came bouncing down the hillside on the end of the rope and caught me a thud on the bottom. I wished that donkey to Hades.

Perhaps she ought to be mated, Charles said later that evening. Transportation in ball and chain was more to my way of thinking at the moment, but there was something, when one considered it, in his suggestion. She was old enough now. It was springtime and the sap was rising. Not only might a foal be perhaps what she was wanting to steady her ... but the idea of a foal, wobbly-legged among the buttercups ... a foal, smaller even than Annabel, nestled in the straw in the stable... Wonderful, I said with dewy eyes. So we set about looking for a mate.

It was August before we found him and he wasn't quite what we'd planned. Our chief difficulty had been transport. There was a donkey named Gentleman at Maidenhead, for instance — handsome, well-bred and a tremendous success with the ladies. He was out of the running because to hire a horsebox to take Annabel to him would have cost — at a shilling a mile for two return journeys, one to take her and one to fetch her back — an absolute fortune. There was a donkey named Benjamin at the Siamese hotel at Halstock where Solomon and Sheba went for their holidays — dark he was, with a coat like plush, and when he'd first arrived to brighten their lives the two elderly jenny donkeys owned by the Francises had come galloping into season almost before he was through their paddock gate. Unfortunately there and back to Halstock with the cats was one thing; there and back twice, in a hired horse box, was again another.

A stallion eight miles away at the seaside was suggested white he was, and he'd sired some splendid foals. When his owner said Annabel would have to go over and run with the other donkeys to achieve results, however, Charles turned that down too. Annabel trotting to the sands in a posse harem... Annabel being jostled by the other donkeys... Annabel standing up in a field all night, and she used to a comfortable bed... He paled at the very thought. 'Do her good', I said with feeling, but Charles wouldn't hear of it. At which point I spotted an advertisement in a paper for horses for sale and a Shetland pony at stud some fifteen miles away and, thinking it might be a dealer, I rang the number at once.

Had they by any chance a donkey at stud as well? I enquired.

They hadn't. Actually it was a breeding establishment for racehorses. But the owner had recently bought a black Shetland mare for his daughter, aged four, and being in the business he hadn't been able to resist a black Shetland stallion to go with her. Peter, having got Gilly successfully in foal, was now at stud for other Shetland mares. What about crossing him with our donkey? The breeder suggested helpfully.

Charles said no to that, too. Then I reminded him of Henry. A jennet, yes. But beautiful, gentle — and, when one considered it, with a definite advantage. We wanted to keep this foal as a companion for Annabel. She wouldn't tolerate a filly when it grew up, that was certain. No competition was Annabel's motto. Equally certain was that we couldn't keep a jack donkey with us for ever — mating back with Annabel and Miss Wellington being scandalised; breaking out to visit the local mares and little mules being born like ninepins... A jennet, I said, was the answer.

After he'd consulted the nearest Veterinary school and been assured that there was nothing wrong about the proposal ... Annabel wouldn't have a Frankenstein ... just a small black jennet with a mane and tail like a Shetland, a temperament like Mum's and the general appearance of a Thelwell pony, Charles thought maybe it was the answer too. *If* we could bring it off, the experts warned him. They wouldn't like to bet on our chances. Ponies didn't always take to donkeys, particularly if they had mares of their own. Any pony would take to *Annabel*, Charles informed them. And so the match was arranged.

We took her over one afternoon. We'd already met Peter ourselves and decided that she'd like him. When we'd gone to the stud-farm previously, however, it had been evening, and Peter, penned in a small enclosure for our inspection, had been the only animal we'd seen. Now, as we unlatched the horsebox, we looked around us. At mares with foals in the paddock, yearlings galloping like Pegasus across a field, a palomino watching us haughtily over a gate... Thoroughbreds, every one of them. Pretty small we felt, unloading a pint-sized donkey from a horsebox in the middle of that lot.

So did the Irish groom detailed to take charge of Annabel. 'Me?' he exclaimed with horror when the breeder, saying we might as well try her now, told him to take her into the yard. 'Groom to a donkey!' he declared tragically to the onlookers as he led her through the gate. 'If they hear of this at Newmarket!' he lamented as Peter was brought out of his stall.

There was no inferiority complex about Annabel. We'd noticed before how she could assume dignity to suit the occasion, and she was certainly dignified now. She stood there like a queen. A distinctly affronted queen, we gathered from the rigidity of her attitude. In front of all these People! Signified the disapproving angle of her ears. What was going on behind was nothing to do with *her*, declared the determinedly detached expression on her face.

That being her outlook, there was in fact nothing going on at all. Peter was keen enough, but nobody can love an ice-maiden.

'Bit fat, of course', commented the breeder poking her speculatively in the stomach. Annabel didn't move an inch, but she'd noted it, I knew from her ears. I hoped, for his own sake, the breeder wouldn't turn his back to her while she was there.

'We'll try her again tomorrow', he finally decided. So we went home and left her there. We drove, with a noticeably silent horse box behind us, telling ourselves that she'd be back with us by the weekend. But that was where we were wrong.

Ten: Annie Mated

It was more than five weeks before we saw Annabel again. Five weeks during which we rang up every other day, the breeder reported nothing doing, and we almost gave up hope.

According to those who know, donkeys and horses come into season at three-weekly intervals. She must have been in season when she arrived, said the breeder, otherwise Peter wouldn't have been interested. She might have been going off then, of course — but how she'd managed to stay off for five weeks afterwards, with Peter around to excite her, was a mystery to him.

It wasn't to us. Sheba had once managed to catch, with exactly a five-week interval, an infection from Solomon which the Vet had said *she* couldn't possibly get after twenty-one days. She'd stopped us from going on holiday on that occasion. Our animals were experts at confounding Science.

All was well now, however. Annabel had at last succumbed to Peter's charms. Twice, two days following, the breeder reported proudly over the telephone. There was no doubt about it now. And so we fetched her home.

She was out at grass with Peter and Gilly when we went over to collect her. A strong companionship had sprung up between the trio, based no doubt on their common diminutiveness, and the two small Shetlands accompanied her loyally across two large fields to the gate when we led her away. Oddly enough it was Gilly who walked closest to her, side by side, apparently her dearest friend. Peter plodded behind, with them but obviously out of things, in the manner of men the world over accompanying a couple of females on a shopping trip.

They watched through the gate as we loaded her into the horse box. They were still watching, two small black figures no bigger than Annabel herself, as we drove out through the yard. It was surprising how other animals took to her, we said. We wondered what Annabel thought?

What Annabel thought was apparent when we got her home. There was a pout on her mouth for days. All she'd gone through, she reminded us, assuming a wilted lily expression every time we spoke to her. She couldn't in her condition, she protested when we tried to hurry her through her gate. Wasn't surprising, she snorted indignantly when we commented how much thinner she was.

It was nice to have her back, all the same. Robertson, who'd vanished while she was away, reappeared like a ginger genie, sitting proprietarily in her stable door though definitely not speaking to me. The rooks were in force again. We'd fed them during her absence but there seemed even more of them about when Annabel was at home.

'The pregnant Valley', said Janet, dreamily tickling Annabel's ears a few days before her own baby was due. 'How wonderfully peaceful it is.'

She didn't say that the next time she came to see us. It was an evening a fortnight later and Janet, leaving Jim keeping an eye on the baby, had dropped in for a first-time-out chat.

'Sherry?' I asked, and Janet said yes, she would. Wonderful she felt, she said, lying back in our biggest armchair. The son and heir at home in his cot; her sitting here without feeling like a hippopotamus; her first glass of sherry in nine whole months...

At that moment there was a blood-curdling scream from the yard. Solomon! I thought, the usual range of possibilities flashing like a film through my mind. Solomon — caught on the roof by Robertson, bitten by an adder he'd mistaken for a slow-worm, attacked (I turned cold at the prospect) by a stoat that he'd met up with and tried to fight...

'I can't go,' I said, my knees turning to jelly as usual. It was obvious that Janet couldn't go, either. She sat there as if turned to stone, her glass half-raised in her hand, while Charles rushed to the kitchen, shouted back that Solomon had caught a hare and I, my knees miraculously recovering themselves, dashed after Charles to see.

I forgot Janet in the excitement of the next few minutes. Solomon had indeed brought home a hare. Knowing him we knew he couldn't have caught it in the ordinary way, of course. We decided later that he must have fallen over it while it was asleep. The hare — a young, inexperienced half-grown one — had most likely been asleep on the hillside; Solomon had probably stumbled over it as he ambled along; and, grabbing it while both he and the hare were in a state of semi-consciousness, he'd brought it home for us to see.

The hare, screaming with fright, was now running round and round the kitchen and Solomon was bounding exuberantly after it as if chivvying a captured mouse. All his quarries were as big as this, we were given to understand, and he could round it up any time he chose...

Even as we debated how to rescue it, however, the hare found the open doorway and was gone. Out across the yard towards the gate and straight, in its panic, into the goldfish pond. Fortunately we keep a net over the pond to ward off herons and in the next split-second sequence the hare rebounded off the net with a mighty splash and was away through the gate to safety.

We could have bet on it, of course. A second later there was another almighty splash. Solomon, in his excitement, had also gone straight into the pond and bounced off the net. By the time *he* got to the gate, the hare was out of sight.

The yard was soaked, Solomon was soaked, we were soaked... It was all right, we assured Janet as we went back into the sitting-room. It was only a hare, and he'd managed to get away. She regarded us from the armchair. It was at that moment that I realised she hadn't moved an inch since we'd left. She was still sitting there like a statue, her glass half-raised in her hand. One thing she knew, she said when we finally convinced her that nobody had been murdered or run amok and that of the three of us, wet though we were, only Solomon had actually fallen in... One thing she knew was that it was no good coming to *us* expecting peace and relaxation.

It certainly wasn't. Only a few weeks later there we were, quietly minding our own business, and before we knew what was happening we were tangled up with the hunt. Normally, when we hear the horn, we get the cats in, make sure Annabel is where she can't frighten the horses, and leave it at that. This time, however, it was the first hunt of the season, they were using some new young hounds, and by the time the hunt was over and the fox had vanished deftly into the woods, they'd lost some of them. Five and a half couples according to the huntsman, who by this time had exchanged his horse for a van in order to search for them. If we came across them, would we hold them?

Translated, five and a half couples is eleven. The question of how we'd hold eleven excited young foxhounds if they did come into our orbit quite escaped us. Feeling sorry for the lost ones, we said we would — though in the event the one we did catch was more than enough.

Actually it wasn't so much that we caught her as that she gave herself up. We were returning from shutting in Annabel for the night when a lemon-and-white figure padded up to us in the dusk, performed a couple of ingratiating squirms, and announced that she was lost. We brought her into the garden, gave her a couple of biscuits, and wondered what to do next. Her own suggestion, when she found we didn't have the rest of the pack in the garden, was that she should jump the wall and go on looking for them. So we put her, as we didn't have a dog-leash, on Annabel's halter.

Janet said later she wondered if she was seeing things when she looked out of her window that afternoon and saw, through the fast-falling darkness, what appeared to be me streaking past with the Hound of the Baskervilles. It was me all right. No sooner had we got the hound on the makeshift leash than we heard the horn further up the valley and Charles said if I ran (he couldn't run on account of his back, he said) I would catch the huntsman and it would save us a lot of trouble.

When I got there, of course, the huntsman had gone. The next thing I heard was the blasted horn sounding, like the horn of Roland, from the heights way above the Valley, where he'd driven in five minutes in his van but it would take me an hour to reach on foot.

Back at the cottage, having been towed down the Valley by the excited hound faster than I remembered running in years, I found Charles in a similar condition of status quo. Having telephoned the hunt kennels and got no reply, Charles had next phoned the local policeman, who was having his tea, and who'd advised him to phone the hunt kennels. 'That's all I could do myself, you see Zur,' said Constable Coggins, helpfully giving Charles the hunt kennels number and hanging up fast before his kipper got cold. So Charles had once more phoned the hunt kennels, once more got no reply, and was sitting there frustratedly demanding what things were coming to.

As if in answer, the hound, whom I'd left tied to the lilac tree while I went in to talk to Charles, at that moment started baying. A forlorn, full-throated call that was like the wind in Fingal's Cave. 'Lo-oooost,' she moaned mournfully down the Valley. 'Tied up in a place where there's no-oooo meat, only bissss-cuits. Come to the rescue at o-ooooonce!'

Refusing to be quiet unless someone stayed with her — and of course we couldn't have her indoors on account of the cats — what happened was that I spent the next three-quarters of an hour sitting on the porch-mat comforting her. She, deciding that she liked being comforted, climbing affectionately on to my lap, Charles put the porch-light on so that the huntsman could see us if he came past and Solomon and Sheba immediately got up into the window that looked on to the porch and, craning their necks so that they could look down at us, started bellowing indignantly themselves at my traitorous behaviour.

The neighbours must have thought they were seeing things that night, the way their homecoming cars slowed, took in the floodlit tableau on our doorstep, and proceeded thoughtfully on up the lane. Never was I more glad than when the hunt van stopped outside our gate, the voice of the huntsman called through the darkness 'Thank goodness you've got our Emily', and Emily, without so much as a parting lick, leapt thankfully over the wall to join him.

Father Adams's comment, when we told him about it, was that it showed how careful we had to be. Whether he meant careful about taking on strange hounds or careful about people seeing me act peculiarly on the porch I wasn't quite sure, but it didn't make much difference anyway. However careful we were things always happened to us. Take, for instance, the episode of Charles's tooth.

When one of his side teeth collapsed while he was eating a nut, the dentist suggested he had a plate. A normal occurrence, many people have them, and Charles's tooth, on the thinnest cobalt plate imaginable, was most realistic. After his initial attempt at eating with it, when he announced that meals now meant nothing to him, never again would he be able to taste anything, he settled down with it very well. The one exception being that when he'd had it in for long periods — particularly when he'd had a hard day at the office or been to visit his Aunt Ethel — it gave him indigestion. He said it did, anyway. He got a strong metallic taste in his stomach.

We were coming back from town one night, even more harassed than usual on account of we'd not only been visiting Aunt Ethel but were extremely worried because we'd lost some keys that morning and couldn't think where they were, when Charles said he'd have to take his tooth out. He couldn't stand it a moment longer, he said. His stomach was sending up signals of solid aluminium.

If he put it in his pocket, I warned him, sure as eggs were eggs he'd lose it. Don't be silly, of course he wouldn't, said Charles, slipping the fragile metal strapping into a fold of his breast pocket handkerchief. After which we forgot about his tooth and returned to worrying about the keys.

We had reason for worrying, too. We could get into the cottage all right; I had a spare key in my handbag. But the garage key was missing, without which we could neither put the car away nor get the hay for Annabel's supper. The coalhouse key was missing, without which we couldn't light the fire. The toolhouse key was missing, which meant if anything went wrong and needed fixing — as, in the circumstances, it undoubtedly would within the hour — Charles couldn't get the tools to do it with.

What with that and our normal homecoming routine of letting out the cats, getting Annabel in, switching on the radio to hear the news, changing used earth-boxes and seeing that Solomon didn't get up the path and encounter Robertson, we were in our usual state of pandemonium.

I searched the bedroom for the keys, and the pockets of Charles's duffle coat. I looked in the dustbin, where they'd been found on several previous occasions, but they weren't there this time. Charles was wandering about the paddock with a torch. Some hope, I thought, he had of finding anything in that mud.

I knew from his tread as he came down the path a while later that the news wasn't good. Honestly, I said. Where things *went* around this place I didn't know. We couldn't feed Annabel, couldn't light the fire, where Solomon had got to I hadn't the vaguest clue…

Solomon was by the rain-barrel, said Charles. He'd passed him coming in. He'd found the keys, he informed me as he kicked off his boots — adding, when I started to say but that was good, 'But now I've lost my tooth.'

He had, too. We searched for it for ages. Upstairs. Downstairs. In the mud of the paddock. Even — since that was where he'd discovered the keys by seeing them glint in the torchlight — in the straw in Annabel's stable. We found it at last where it must have fallen when Charles bent to switch on the radio. On the rug in front of the fireplace. We'd have trodden on it long before if Solomon, presumably under the impression that it was some sort of spider, hadn't been sitting there cautiously keeping an eye on it. Meanwhile, being used to Solomon and his trophy hunting, we'd been stepping over and around him automatically, and had never noticed a thing. It was only when he reached out and cautiously poked it that I realised what our fat man was watching. There was no dignity around this place, said Charles, leaping to the rescue of his beloved tooth just as Solomon's paw came stealthily up for the kill. Just no dignity at all.

Eleven: How to Light an Aga

Things were quiet after that until Christmas. Reasonably quiet, that is. There was one little upheaval when the Parish Council, having met and discussed the complaint about Mr Carey's entrance, duly announced its decision in the matter, which was to refer it to the County Council. This meant another two months before the reply could itself be debated and that, with luck, the matter would still be under discussion in six months' time.

When this state of affairs was reported back to the Rose and Crown, Fred Ferry said if 'twere he he'd put weed-killer on th'eather and have done with it. Actually Fred wouldn't have done any such thing. It was just his way of talking. This being precisely what had occasioned his previous row with Father Adams, however — Father Adams having planted a privet hedge against the boundary wire because he fancied it, Fred Ferry saying the roots would spoil his dahlias and making a cryptic reference to weed-killer, the hedge having subsequently died and Father Adams having dark suspicions as to how it had happened — from then on Father Adams was on the side of Mr C.

Some people was a mite too handy with their weedkiller, he announced in the general direction of the bottom of his cider mug. Some people wanted to mind their dahlias didn't go instead of th'eather. Why *shouldn't* the chap have a heather bank if he wanted to? demanded Father Adams, coming up for air, banging down his mug, and warming more and more, the more he thought of it, to the idea of an Englishman's cottage being his castle and if he wanted to block up his entrance and grow heather on it, why the Magna Carta shouldn't he?

'What about the beer lorry then?' asked Fred indignantly. Father Adams said 'What about it?' back — adding, in the heat of the moment and in complete negation of his former attitude, that it ought to be *made* to unload at the front door, sticking there blocking the roadway like that — and thereby he sealed his fate for weeks.

The supporters of the Rose and Crown to a man weren't speaking to him. Father Adams, for his part, went stubbornly out of his way to talk to Mr Carey whenever he saw him. He was also, when he wanted a drink, going over to the Horse and Hounds in the next village for it, and the sight of Father Adams in our car headlights, trudging defiantly along the lane in the wrong direction as we came home at night, gave us as much a feeling of unreality as did the occasions on which we'd seen a badger in the self-same spot.

The atmosphere down with us was much more harmonious. It was the mouse-catching season, for a start. Afternoons saw Sheba ensconced beside the fish-pool, gazing prettily at a hole in the bottom of the woodshed, warmed by the autumn sunshine and nicely handy for a chat with passers-by. Solomon did his mousing in the garden path. A sunken path which runs from the cottage to the garage, with nine-inch high stone walls on either side. His mouse-hole was in one of the walls. Watching it in his case meant not sitting close to it as Sheba did — patiently, scarcely breathing except when a passing admirer spoke to her, when, being Sheba, she forgot and bawled enthusiastically back. Watching it in Solomon's case meant an ambush position three feet away against the opposite wall. To delude the mouse into coming out, we understood. He hadn't found Sheba's method very successful.

As his interpretation of Sheba's method had been to sit bang in front of a hole, breathe down it, peer down it, and, when all else failed, put his paw down it in an effort to liven things up, we appreciated this new development. Solomon, we said, was actually *thinking*.

It was a pity he had to choose the path to put his deductions into practice, though. In order not to disturb him, we now couldn't walk up it. Mustn't come between a cat and his mouse-hole, must we? Charles called encouragingly' across to him as we took our new route to the garage — up the path as usual to begin with; a wide, semi-circular detour across the lawn at the point of operation; and then rejoining the path further on.

It was all very well in daylight, but when Charles did it one night in the dusk he fell over the snowberry bush. Even in daylight it had its drawbacks, too. Our garden is low-walled and open to the public gaze. The path being sunken, people looking in as they passed — as, in the country, they invariably do — couldn't see Solomon sitting in it mouse-watching. All they could see was us, apparently bonkers at last, proceeding in mysterious semi-circles over the lawn.

It was peaceful, nevertheless. Sheba by the woodshed; Solomon in the path; Robertson, with a defiantly turned back indicating no connection with anybody, hunting all by himself in the paddock hedge.

All was peaceful with Annabel, too. It had been Janet's idea to take her waist measurement when she came back from being mated. Owing to their being barrel-shaped it is very difficult to tell when donkeys are in foal — but this way, said Janet inspiredly, we couldn't go wrong. Measure her now … measure her in six months' time … the difference would be bound to show.

We measured her. Fifty-four inches. We looked at her incredulously. Fifty-four inches *now*, when to our eyes she looked quite thin? What must she have been before? we wondered. And what, if one could encompass such expansion, would she measure when her time was up?

Fifty-four feet, judging by the way she was eating. 'Eating for two, remember!' said Miss Wellington coyly, whose chief occupation these days seemed to be making Yorkshire Puddings, having a spoonful herself, and bringing the remainder down to Annabel to keep up her strength. It wasn't just the amount that was suspicious, either. Annabel was eating nettles. Fresh ones from the hedgerows, dusty ones from the edges of the lane, dried-up old dead ones from the bonfire heap where they'd been put for burning and were pulled out and eaten by Annabel as she passed as if she would die on the spot without them. Seeing that she'd previously declared nettles were poison and she'd die on the spot if she ate them, we were certain that something was up. So we were when Annabel fell down. Sure-footed, nimble as a goat, with legs like little stool-props on which she *couldn't* fall down, she was going up the lane when she did. A step or two up the bank to reach a dandelion and there she was, a typical expectant mother, rolling helplessly on her back in the dust.

We helped her up, felt her anxiously and decided that all was well. It was a sign though, we said. From then on we were more careful. Walked either side of her when we took her uphill. Tethered her on the lawn when the ground was frozen so she couldn't trip over things. Which was one of the reasons why, that year, we had a somewhat eventful Christmas.

It began with the Hazells going to London. Over Christmas itself this time, to visit their parents. *If we* could feed Rufus, said Janet hesitantly, and keep the Aga going till Boxing

Night…? Of course we would, we said warmly. No trouble at all. So Jim fixed the Aga to burn more slowly — that way, he said, we need stoke it only once a day; he knew we'd be busy with visitors — and off, waving happily, they went.

I'd said not to touch that Aga. We were going up twice a day in any case to feed Rufus. We weren't experts at Agas ourselves. I'd have felt much safer doing it twice a day, as we'd always done in the past.

It was all right the first night. The Aga was doing well. Next morning — Christmas Eve — it was noticeably cooler. I filled it, riddled it furiously and hoped for the best. That night it was out. Charles, the super-optimist, insisted that it wasn't. Riddle it, he said, suiting his action to the words; open the bottom; in ten minutes it would be going like a bomb. Ten minutes later Rufus said it wasn't any warmer, was it? and Charles said he'd think of something. Meanwhile we took Rufus up a hot-water bottle.

I got little sleep that night. Charles's Aunt Ethel, who was staying with us for Christmas, never sleeps properly away from home as she is always telling us. What with listening to her bed springs creaking restlessly through the wall, her getting out of bed, her getting back again — after which, with the same sort of relief one gets from hearing the fall of the second boot, I *ought* to have been able to doze off only I was stark-eyed worrying about the Aga — I heard every hour strike till dawn.

To add to everything we'd had a heavy frost. The Aga out, the house getting colder, the Hazells coming home to a heatless Boxing Night — visions whirred through my mind like Cinemascope. When I got to the weather turning to snow, the Hazells being delayed, the pipes bursting and the carpets being ruined, I woke Charles in a panic. Nonsense, said Charles reassuringly. We'd get it going easily now we knew it was out.

All we needed was some charcoal. What he'd overlooked, of course, was that it was now Christmas Day and we couldn't get any.

I will draw a veil over the events of the day that followed, save to say that at our party that night the chief topic was how to start Agas. Coal, suggested someone. If we stood by and watched it? In the intervals of cooking the turkey we'd tried that all the morning. Firelighters, suggested another. If we used enough of them? In between cutting sandwiches we'd tried those all the afternoon. Charcoal, insisted an expert; you couldn't use anything else. We gave him a nasty look.

It was colder than ever that night. The glass was dropping. The ground rang like iron when we saw our guests off and Rufus shivered visibly when we took up another hot-water bottle. Even Charles was wakeful when we went to bed, and at four in the morning he informed me that he had solved it.

We have one of those air-controlled open fires. A big one, with plenty of draught. Get our fire going like a smithy, said Charles; bring down some of the Aga fuel and lay it in rows on top; then he'd go up and empty the Aga, when he'd done he'd phone me at the cottage, I would then shovel the red-hot fuel into a bucket and run up the lane with it (I do an awful lot of running when you come to think of it), pour it into the empty stove, and Bob would be our uncle.

Surprisingly enough he was, though it was a good thing nobody actually saw me on my mission, heading hot-foot up the lane with the makings of a rattling good forest fire.

It was an old bucket with leaky seams. Running increased the draught and it was glowing like a brazier as I panted through the Hazell's door. Into the kitchen, down through the funnel, more fuel piled on top as fast as we could shovel it…

It worked. The world was a different place an hour later as we strolled back down the Valley. Behind us was a rapidly warming house, a tidied kitchen, a purring ginger cat sitting happily on the cover of the hot plate. Before us lay the rest of Boxing Day in which to relax. To chat to Aunt Ethel, pay some attention to the animals, go over to Charles's brother in the evening…

We'd left Annabel tethered on the lawn with some hay. We'd been a bit worried because the lawn was extra icy but she had to have an airing. It was alarming, nevertheless, to get back and find that her rope was broken.

We really must get a stronger one, I said, grabbing the end and anchoring her hastily to the lilac tree. Supposing she'd realised she was loose? Galloped up the lane after us in her condition and slipped on the icy track? I wilted, I said, at the thought. At that moment Aunt Ethel came scuttling round the corner in a salmon pink dressing gown and brogues and I wilted in earnest. Aunt Ethel, who is over eighty, never goes outside the door, even to the dustbin, without her hat and coat. Something was obviously up.

Had been up, to be correct. It seemed that Annabel, annoyed at our going off without her, had broken her tether rope shortly after I'd left and had followed me up the lane. Aunt Ethel, gazing peacefully out on the winter landscape before going up to dress, had seen her and given chase in dressing gown and slippers. Unable to catch her, and miraculously not having fallen down herself, she'd come back with the intention of ringing us at the Hazells, but realised she didn't know the number. Unearthing the directory (what on earth, she said, induced us to keep it in the log box?) she found there were an awful lot of Hazells, and some of them spelt it with an 's'. She'd decided it was probably 'z', started to go through the list, had a couple of interesting conversations with people whom she'd apparently addressed as Charles and told them the donkey was loose — they, she said indignantly, hadn't known what she was talking about, which was hardly surprising when we looked up the directory later and discovered that the first one lived twenty miles away and the second one nearer forty... 'And then', she said, fixing me with a look, 'your Aunt rang up'.

My Aunt Louisa has an affinity for trouble. Let her clear a table and you can guarantee she'll drop the tray. Put her on a bus for us and you can bet she'll go past the stop. How she could have mucked things up by telephone was beyond all comprehension, but true to form, she had. Aunt Ethel, explaining about Annabel, had asked if she knew how Hazell was spelt. With an 's' or a 'z'? Louisa, who didn't know and had never met them, always likes to be helpful. 'With an 's',' she declared unhesitatingly.

Aunt Ethel abandoned the Hazells, went through — to their complete mystification — the list of fifteen Hasells, and was mentally wringing Louisa's neck before restarting on the 'z's' when she happened to glance out of the window and there, on the lawn, having reappeared with the suddenness of a magician's rabbit, was Annabel. Having failed to find us, she'd come back to finish her breakfast.

Stopping only to put on her brogues — as a precaution, she said, against slipping — Aunt Ethel had sallied forth to tie her up and that was where we'd come in. It was just as well we had. If Aunt Ethel *had* laid hands on the rope — and if Annabel had started cavorting, as she usually does if she thinks it's loose — our aged relation would have gone across the lawn like a water-skier on those solid, thick-soled brogues.

We escorted her inside, gave her some whisky, had some ourselves to calm our nerves. 'Anything exciting happen?' asked Jim Hazell, ringing up next morning to thank us for seeing to the Aga. Nothing exceptional, said Charles reflectively. Not when you considered it was us.

Twelve: Vitamins for Everybody

Actually it proved a season of alarms. First of all I thought Sheba had kidney trouble. We'd heard of a cat which did have it and we knew the symptoms, and when I noticed Sheba going continually to the water-bowl one day my heart sank in my shoes. Either kidneys or diabetes, said the cat-book when I looked up excessive water-drinking, and that raised another possibility. Diabetic people put on weight.

Sheba was plumper lately. We'd put it down to her current passion for cream off the milk. As we'd attributed that in turn to her being unable any longer to watch Solomon drinking it alone — slurp, slap, guzzle he went, and if you can't stop the racket do it yourself, that way you don't hear it so much, we'd thought was Sheba's reasoning — it hadn't struck us as very significant. The question now was, however, was she plump because of diabetes, or was she drinking milk because she had kidney trouble and was thirsty?

Neither, as a matter of fact. It was the salt I'd put in their rabbit. When, after I'd been worrying over her for hours, Solomon came down from his morning nap under our eiderdown, joined her at the water-bowl and, taking it in like a suction pump, drank half the bowl at once, it suddenly came to me. Someone had said salt was good for them and the previous day, for the first time ever, I'd tried it out. Sprinkled it on their rabbit in the pressure cooker. A little too liberally it now appeared, but at least everybody's kidneys were in order.

Annabel didn't die of eating bacon-rind either, which was our next domestic hiatus. She ate a lot of peculiar things these days including the goldfish food, which we discovered her sucking surreptitiously off the surface of the pond under guise of having a drink. That, however, was biscuit meal and harmless. Apart from making sure the fish didn't vanish as well, we didn't worry about it.

We wouldn't have worried about the bacon rind except that it was just our luck, the morning she ate it, there'd been a talk on the wireless about donkeys. Yew trees and meat were fatal to them, warned the speaker, at which we'd raised our eyebrows superiorly. Yew trees, yes. We'd heard of animals dropping dead with sprigs still in their mouths. But meat... Donkeys wouldn't *touch* it, we said, with memories of a hiker once giving Annabel a ham sandwich and Annabel spluttering it indignantly back at him.

That was at breakfast time. Within half an hour that donkey had come into the yard, gone over the flagstones with lips questing as inquisitively as an elephant's trunk as was her wont, gathered up all the birds' crumbs as was her wont also, now that she was eating for two — and scoffed while she was at it, all the bacon-rind.

She'd never touched it before, but deciding that it was her condition didn't help much during the vigil that followed. We dared not ring Mr Harler. A leg of lamb, yes. Four pieces of bacon rind — no. There was a limit to the situations with which we could confront him. We sweated it out ourselves.

Two hours later, with Annabel still on her feet, Charles said it was obviously all right if it was cooked. Maybe it was, but we took no more chances. After that the bacon rind was put out of her reach on the bird-table, and on the occasions when she came into the kitchen we made sure the refrigerator door was shut so she couldn't get at anything raw.

We had no illusions about her nosing it out otherwise, if we felt like it. She'd been coming into the kitchen since she was a foal, and it held no mysteries for her. She knew as well as we did that sugar came out of the bottom cupboard, apples were in a bowl on the dresser and it was Nice if you stood by the convector. Lately she stood by it more than ever. It was good for Julius, she informed us — Julius being the expected foal, so-called because we anticipated him in July.

There were times, of course, when, while it was convenient to have Annabel in the yard, because we knew then where she was, it wasn't convenient to have her in the kitchen. When we had visitors, for instance, and they might not have fancied little donkeys sniffing at the saucepans, or if I wasn't there myself to keep an eye on what she was doing. On such occasions I used to shut her out. It was no use that winter. It was so wet that the door swelled with the dampness and, as Annabel soon discovered, the lock developed a habit of sticking. One biff with her head, open it would fly and in, with a triumphant snort, would come Annabel to warm Julius some more. The only remedy was to bolt the door — which, if I did, resulted in the cottage being shaken to its foundations as Annabel determinedly rammed it, and my rushing to open it anyway, before Julius came loose from his moorings.

Unfortunately it wasn't only Annabel who could open the door. Solomon could do it too, tugging from the inside with his incredibly powerful claws. Try as I might to make sure it was firmly shut, the moment I left it Solomon would rake and claw and howl and roar until a sudden ominous silence would inform us that he'd done it again. Forced the door and was away on trouble bent.

It was as a result of this that eventually he had his last great fight with Robertson. Finding the door open I'd gone out to check on him as usual. I'd looked. Listened. There was no sign of anybody. No howl for help. No sound of battle. He must, I decided, have gone up behind the cottage where Robertson never went. He was safe up there and the air would do him good. Even Solomon had been indoors a lot during the recent awful weather…

He'd gone up behind the cottage all right — and so, for once, had his enemy. When Solomon came back a while later he had the most dreadful fight wounds I have ever seen on a cat. His ears were bleeding, his stomach gouged by ripping claws, his paws so savagely bitten that the bites went right through his pads. But for the mud and the smell, where Robertson had apparently rolled him on the ground and sprayed him in defeat, and the tell-tale fur-tufts, ginger and Siamese mixed, that lay like drifts of dandelion clocks where they'd met and fought under the rowan tree, I'd have thought he'd met up with a fox.

The fight had been so fiendish that that was obviously why it had been so silent. Nobody had had the breath to howl. The smell was fiendish, too. Solomon reeked like a Venetian canal. I sponged him as best I could without disturbing him, but when Sheba joined him on the hot-water bottle that night, just when our wounded warrior was at his lowest ebb and Sheba cuddling up to him would have given him comfort, she positively reeled. He Stank, she said, spitting at him and fleeing from the chair in horror.

No Florence Nightingale was Sheba. For days, while Solomon lay in his chair unable to walk, feeding wanly from our hands, struggling weakly to his haunches when he wanted to use his box, which was a signal for us to lift him down, and looking mutely at us when he'd finished, which was the signal to lift him back, Sheba slept relentlessly on the settee. Want her to catch something? she bawled, leaping indignantly from the chair if we tried to put her with him. Want her to smell like that? she demanded, when Charles said why wasn't she kind to him.

Three weeks later, however, when the sequel to the fight occurred, Solomon no longer smelled, Sheba was back to sleeping with him — and that was how our next traumatic drama took place.

We'd had to take Solomon to the Vet. He'd recovered by now from his wounds. He had countless bare patches where they'd been, of course, and eventually, as well we knew, he'd grow white hairs there for a while as a result of the shock. He had done since he was a kitten, this time he was going to look spotted as a rocking horse and Sheba would no doubt start nattering about catching those too, in due course — but it wasn't that that was worrying us.

Solomon was off his food. Badly off his food. As a result of shock, we'd thought at first, or maybe because of his distress at being defeated. Now, three weeks later, he wasn't eating at all; he was thin and light as a feather; and, most ominous of all, we hadn't heard him speak for days.

Vitamin deficiency said Mr Harler when, for the umpteenth time, Solomon once more stood woefully on his surgery table being gone over with thermometer and stethoscope. But wasn't it the same as last year? I suggested anxiously. When Solomon fought Robertson, if he remembered, and caught a virus, and he'd given him aureomycin? It was the aureomycin I wanted to remind him of. By now I was expecting Solomon to collapse at any minute, aureomycin had pulled him round before, and I didn't want any mistake about it.

Mr Harler eyed me sternly. Last time, he said, this cat had had a temperature. This time he didn't. Aureomycin wouldn't have any effect. He didn't have a virus. Maybe this was the result of shock — such deficiency sometimes was — but it was

Vitamin B he needed, and it was Vitamin B he was going to *get*. Saying which he got out a syringe, fixed an ampoule to the end of it, tested it, applied it practisedly to Solomon's rear — and the contents shot straight through the back of the syringe and over Charles.

'Stuck,' said Mr Harler resignedly, obviously wondering how we did it. He fetched another syringe and ampoule, fixed things up again, and this time Solomon got the dose intended for him. Within minutes Mr Harler was seeing us relievedly off from the surgery steps, telling us to let him know tomorrow if he wasn't any better but he thought that would do the trick.

It did so far as Solomon was concerned. He ate some meat from my hand as soon as he got home. He was wolfing food the next morning as if we'd been starving him for a month. It was the rest of us who suffered.

I'm afraid I wasn't very sympathetic when Charles, driving home from the Vet's, came over queer when we reached the cottage. He'd been nattering so much about the stuff spraying into his mouth and the putrid taste of it and wondering whether it was poisonous or not, that I put it down to his imagination. When, as he went to get out, he suddenly sat heavily on the running-board and said that he felt giddy, I said 'Don't be silly, it didn't make Solomon giddy' and never gave it another thought.

Not till the following day, that was, when we were in the sitting-room just before tea — Solomon, with a solid meal of rabbit inside him, curled recuperatively in the armchair, Sheba spread like a little blue buffalo robe on top of him, and a log-fire blazing comfortingly in the grate. Outside, which made things seem even cosier, it was snowing heavily. A late snowfall we hadn't anticipated, which by now was a good ten inches deep.

'Thank goodness we took Solomon to Harler yesterday,' I said with relief. 'We'd never have got through in this.' Charles agreed; we looked with a common thought towards the chair in which, just at that moment, Sheba was reaching out to give Solomon a loving lick on his flanks — and in that very instant it happened. Sheba leapt from the chair before our eyes, gnashed her teeth in frenzy and, foaming alarmingly at the mouth, started tearing round and round the room.

'She's having a fit!' I whispered, almost too scared to speak. 'How can we get her to Harler?' cried Charles, his thoughts on the impassable roads. And there we were once more like a scene from Tchekov. The snow slanting down outside, Sheba going round and round in circles, Charles and I wringing our hands and Solomon — visible only as a pair of big round eyes — hiding under the table.

It came to us eventually, of course. That some of the spilt injection must have gone over Solomon's coat, that Sheba had just licked it off and that — allowing for the fact that Charles hadn't actually foamed at the mouth or run in circles himself (a lot of notice I'd have taken if he had, he said, when I wouldn't even believe he'd been feeling giddy) her reaction had been much the same as his. We caught her, wiped the taste from her mouth with a towel, and in seconds she'd recovered. Except — trust Sheba — that when she tried to tell Charles about it, thanks to all the frothing she'd done and all the lick she'd lost, nothing came out but a squeak.

Meanwhile the snow came implacably down; Solomon spoke for the first time in weeks, wailing from under the table that he was Convalescent if we remembered, and he'd like some food if we'd finished playing; and our lives returned to normal.

More normal than they'd been for a long time, for in the interim Robertson had been adopted. By a family new to the district who wanted a cat and who, when they heard the story of our ginger outcast, offered to give him a home. It was the only possible solution. Sorry for him as we were, we couldn't have kept him any longer, with his terrible hatred for Solomon. So Robertson — fed, sheltered and with a family at last to call his own — went to live at the top of the hill, and we, with Solomon and Sheba, returned to peace once more in the Valley.

For a little while, at any rate. No sooner was Solomon on his feet and out again than we heard, one day, the old familiar war-cry from the hillside. 'Robertson!' we cried in unison, making as one for the door.

It wasn't Robertson. It was a strange black cat who, after one close-up howl from Solomon, fled for his life into the trees. We grabbed Solomon, brought him back, set him down, with warnings about fighting, in the yard... It was no use, of course. Solomon — King of the Valley again what with Mr Harler's vitamins, a successful wrestling bout or two with Sheba and now this strange cat running away from him, was back up on the hillside like a longshot.

I was up there like a longshot after him, too, and so it was that I was on hand when Annabel, grazing blissfully a dozen yards or so away, suddenly decided to charge him. Only in fun, no doubt, seeing that everybody else seemed to be running after him and there he was so temptingly standing on a tussock. But Solomon had his back to her — and Annabel, these days, was temperamentally unpredictable.

There was no time to get between them. At top speed I raced after her, gave her a push from behind that sent her flying down the hill away from Solomon, unable to stop myself I went flying down behind her...

Now we were really back to normal said Charles as with Annabel snorting derisively from the pathway and Solomon, calm as a cucumber, still surveying the land for the other cat from his tussock, I retrieved myself from a clump of nettles.

Thank goodness, indeed we were.

Thirteen: Comes the Spring

The trouble between Father Adams and Fred Ferry resolved itself around this time, too. Quite simply through Father Adams's television set catching on fire. If they'd thought of it somebody could have arranged it afore, said a wit in the Rose and Crown that night when, after their vicissitudes of the past few months, the pair of them sat sheepishly quaffing their cider side by side at the table by the fire.

But nobody had thought of it, and it had taken spontaneous combustion on the part of the ancient set while Father Adams was, as Fred kept joyfully informing his audience, 'Out in the little old outhouse', to bring about the desired reunion. Fred, passing by and seeing the flames, had rushed into the house and pulled out the plug. Mr Carey had rushed in after him and smothered the fire with a rug, which explained why the third member of the trio at the table, looking more sheepish even than the other two and assuring everybody who spoke to him that it was only ginger ale he was drinking, was the Rose and Crown's erstwhile bête noir.

Not any more, though. The brewery-men had long grown accustomed to taking the beer through the other door which, to tell the truth, was more convenient. The fact that the heather had taken root on his banks showed Mr Carey to be a man who knew his gardening. The County Council's decision not only that it was legal for him to alter his entrance if he wished but that people who used his entrance for passing in were in point of fact committing trespass, proved that he knew his rights (and of nobody does a country-dweller approve more heartily than the man who knows those). All it needed was something like the fire to break the ice and there he was. Discussing the best way of planting rhubarb crowns with Alby Smith. Where the new post-box ought to be (as against where the authorities had recently put it) with Harry Freeman. One of the village at last.

As fast as one door closes another opens, however, as Miss Wellington is fond of saying, and never is it truer than in a village. No sooner had that little problem settled itself than the Duggans were in the soup.

It was spring, of course, when ventures start up like snowdrops, so it was hardly surprising when the Duggans woke up one morning in their bungalow on the hilltop to find that someone had started building on the steep, wooded slope below them.

They wouldn't have minded normal building, said Alan Duggan a few days later. Cement mixers and men dropping planks and lorries coming past with piles of bricks — it had happened with their own bungalow and they'd have stood it, in their turn, with other people's. But a *bulldozer*, he said (for the hillside had to be dug out to level the site). Working at *weekends*, he said (for the construction, we soon discovered, was being done by a part-time builder). Working at *night*, he howled, when an arc-light went up while the bulldozer chugged on without respite.

Trees crashed, bonfires blazed, the bulldozer thudded. At intervals the barrage appeared to be intensified by mortar fire which was, Charles happily insisted, old Alan firing back. Actually it was the quarry a mile away blasting rock for the next day's work, but it fitted into the cacophony like the guns in the 1812 Overture.

What really convinced the Duggans that it wasn't their year was when, in the middle of all this, the people on their other side started building a boat. A nice young couple they were, whose cabin cruiser, rising from their driveway like Venus from the foam, roused admiration on the part of all but the local diehards who wanted to know what they wanted it for in the middle of the country, and the Duggans, over the fence, who had to listen to the Seraph being built.

Peaceful as doves for six blasted years and now *they* had to blasted well start, said Alan. He hoped they sank at sea, he muttered savagely, listening night after night to the sawing. It was the hammering, however, that really got him. Hammering which in the normal way he'd never have noticed, but which, added to the clamour of the building, fell on his anguished ears like water torture.

We called on them one Saturday afternoon and heard it ourselves. From one side came the powerful thud of the bulldozer. From the other, gentle, spasmodic tapping.

'You wait a minute,' said Alan sourly. 'In a second she'll start as well.' In a second she did. Rhythmically from over the fence came the sound of Maureen swinging practisedly into beat with Reggie, their hammers clanging merrily as a pair of Clydeside riveters while they dreamed of summer in their cruiser on the Broads. Up from the hillside echoed the shuddering of the bulldozer. Boom! in the background went the quarry detonators.

'Swine!' roared Alan — suddenly, to our consternation, shaking his fist at the ceiling. 'Swinehounds!' he shouted fiercely, rushing out and kicking as hard as he could at the fence. Nobody could hear him, of course, which was just as well for local relationships. He did it every Saturday, his wife explained placidly. It lessened his tensions, he said.

Our tensions at the time were concerned mainly with our septic tank which, for the umpteenth time since we'd bought the cottage, was waterlogged. It was partly the spring, of course. The rain soaking the ground, the streams coming down from the hills, the fact that we lived in the Valley bottom where the water collected naturally. It was also, as we knew from experience, an undoubted fact that our outlet pipes were silted up. Had they been put in steeply sloping, as they should have been, they would have cleared themselves by gravity. Put in practically horizontally, as they were, over a period of time the silt built up, the water couldn't get through, the silt dried out like cement — and, as Sidney, our erstwhile handyman, cheerfully put it, there we were again, bunged up.

Sidney could afford to be cheerful. The last time it had happened he'd been working for us at weekends and had the job of digging down to the pipes himself. Since then, however, Sidney had prospered. Become his ageing builder-employer's right-hand man, drove the lorry, acted as foreman. Sidney was beyond the spare-time clearing of people's drains now, and who could blame him? The snag was, so now he was in charge of it — was Sidney's firm.

'Have to wait a long time afore we'd get down to he,' he informed us, checking off a list of waiting customers as long as the lane. 'You could do 'n *yourself*, though,' he added, as though the thought had suddenly struck him. 'Dig down *here*' — indicating an area under the rockery. 'Rod 'n through *there*' — indicating the line of the pipes under the lawn. 'Do 'n in half a day, as easy as pie.'

On the previous occasion it had taken Sidney a fortnight of spare-time work to get to the pipes, several hours of poking and prodding to clear out the silt, and ourselves (since at that stage Sidney had had enough and we didn't see sign of him for ages) a couple of months of personal endeavour to fill in the hole. Half a day — even though, as Sidney light-heartedly pointed out, we didn't need to dig the pipes right up this time; just find th' end and rod 'em along — seemed optimistic even at that stage. A fortnight later, with a positive slag-heap of earth on the lawn, Charles about eight feet deep down a hole like a churchyard vault and still no sign of the pipes, Charles turned purple when he thought of Sidney.

It wasn't just digging the hole, he said with feeling. It was being down it when people came past. Miss Wellington peering over and asking what he was doing, for instance — to which Charles replied 'Digging a hole'. Father Adams enquiring whether he were practising to be Sexton, then to which Charles's reply was unrepeatable. The Rector coming in to introduce a friend — neither of them apparently the least perturbed about Charles being down below ground level, but what, demanded Charles, must it have looked like?

What it looked like when he wasn't working, with the hole covered with sheets of corrugated iron on which sat two Siamese cats importantly mouse-hunting and, if she could possibly get at it, Annabel climbing the earth-mound for practice on her way back to her stable, was also a matter for speculation.

His most embarrassing moment was my fault, however. It was a Saturday afternoon when Charles, after a particularly frustrating morning, said he wasn't going out again; he'd finished. We'd get another contractor, he said. One out from town if necessary. Him all the time in dirty clothes, he said. People coming by and staring at him. That cat, he said, with a glare at Solomon, getting down the hole and under his feet as fast as he dug it — to which Solomon aggrievedly replied that he didn't want the mice down there biting him, did he?

It was I who said Oh come now, just an inch or two more and he was bound to find the pipe, and if anybody came by he could duck. It was I, therefore, who was responsible for the fact that when a short while later the riding school came past — the only people who, from the backs of their horses, *could* look over the gate and down the hole and see him — Charles was there once more in the bottom of the trench.

It was a good thing he was, because at that moment he noticed something he hadn't seen before. Two feet up from the floor of the hole, there in the hard-packed earth wall, solid with silt itself which was why we hadn't spotted it, was the round clay rim of the outlet pipe. He'd been digging on beyond it for at least a week.

I didn't know that at the time. All I knew was that I heard voices and looked out to see the riding teacher conversing as imperturbably with Charles, in the bowels of the earth, as if he'd been sitting on a horse at her side, while surrounding her in a parade-style semi-circle, gazing down upon him with the greatest of interest, were ten round-eyed children and their ponies.

I wasn't surprised that his face was red when they'd gone and he clambered out. I forgot that, though, in the excitement of the discovery of the outlet. We fetched the drain-rods; pushed them up the pipes; Charles took off the cover of the septic tank to check the level, at which the cats appeared across the lawn as if by magic... Sheba to be immediately retrieved, wailing that she only wanted to look, from hanging head-first down the septic tank; Solomon to be hauled, howling about the mice he knew were there, from the by now highly vulnerable bottom of the hole. Just in time, too, for a moment later the silt gave way and four feet of drainage water shot into the hole with a roar. The operation, at last, was a success.

It was some days later that I was in the garden when the riding school went by again and the teacher heartily enquired as to whether I was pregnant. 'Huh?' I enquired open-mouthed, sure I must have misheard. 'I said are you PREGNANT?' she shouted. 'ANNABEL I mean,' she yelled as she cantered past.

I said we hoped she was. *Honestly*, I said to Charles when I went indoors. Was my face *red*? Supposing Miss Wellington had heard, or Father Adams, or Janet and Jim? Now I knew why he'd turned red, said Charles resignedly. That was what she'd said to *him*.

Interest in Annabel was growing rapidly now. People kept stopping to ask when she was due to foal; were we going to keep it; what were we going to call it. Our own chief interest was whether it was there at all. We couldn't feel anything or was it significant that when we tried, Annabel walked pettishly away saying she didn't *like* being touched just there. Her waist measurement didn't reveal anything. Fifty-eight inches by now — which, though that, it was interesting to note, was exactly the same circumference as the top of our rain-barrel, was only four inches in seven months beyond normal, and could have been accounted for by the amount of food she'd eaten.

Miss Wellington, purveyor of Yorkshire puddings to Annabel, was sure beyond possible doubt. There was a look on her dear little face, she said. Indigestion, said Charles, sotto voce, and her face was the last thing to go by.

That was the opinion at the farm. Annabel stayed there for a week that spring, while we went for a short sailing holiday. We came back, went up to fetch her, I was discussing the weather with Mrs Pursey… I was holding Annabel on her halter while we talked and I was most surprised when I looked round to see Charles and Farmer Pursey bending down to peer under her stomach.

What they were looking for I hadn't a clue, but Annabel obviously knew. In the middle of the yard. In front of other people. No thought for a donkey's feelings. I knew what that expression meant, as I'd known at the racehorse stable.

'Her teats,' said Charles, when, as we went down the hill, I asked what they had been looking for. 'Farmer Pursey said when they begin to swell it's the surest sign with cows.'

Annabel snorted indignantly when he added that they couldn't find hers at all. Of course they couldn't, she said. She wasn't a cow. She was a Lady.

Fourteen: Putting a Foot in It

As far as her undercarriage was concerned, Annabel went on being a lady. Her teats were there all right, hidden in the thick cream fur that covered her stomach, but they didn't swell. Perhaps with a little donkey they wouldn't, said someone else — or maybe not until she actually foaled.

As the months went by there were other signs, however.

One morning we noticed Annabel, as we thought, looking persistently in at us through the kitchen window — the one that faced on to the yard. She was there when we had our coffee. She was there when I went out to get the lunch, nuzzling round the frame and wasn't she clever, I said, to realise she could watch us through that?

What she was actually doing was eating the putty. Charles had recently renewed it and presumably it still tasted of linseed, but it was an odd thing to do, nevertheless. Other than Charles's anguished outcry when he saw the tooth-marks — that dam blasted donkey ate everything, he said; it was a wonder she didn't eat us — undoubtedly it was significant of something.

So it appeared when, for the first time ever, she jibbed at climbing the steep track up into the Forestry estate. It was safe to let her run free there and normally, full of excitement at going for a walk, she galloped it like a Derby winner — up and back at least six times while we climbed it ourselves, kicking skittishly sideways at us when we laughed. Lately, though, she'd taken to walking it and this time, at the steepest part, she stopped. She sighed, eyed the track and visibly rested. We would have taken her back but for the fact that when we tried to turn her, being Annabel she immediately insisted in going on up. If she stumbled by the wayside we weren't to worry, she assured us. She knew donkeys were only beasts of burden. If Julius fell right out she'd carry on.

Having reached the top without this calamity happening she announced that it was all right this time but now Julius would like some grass, and started grazing. She always did up here, where the grass was green and lush. She'd stay there for hours if we let her, and normally we chivvied her on. This time, however, we left her, slipped quietly round the corner, and continued our walk alone. We'd go just to the gate at the bottom to give Julius time to settle, we decided, and then come back, put her on her halter and take her home. No more up the hill for her, we said. One shock like that was enough.

We got our second shock ten minutes later, when, while we were at the gate, leaning on it and gazing, still sweating slightly, at the scenery, we heard the sound of determinedly galloping hooves. 'Annabel!' I gasped in horror, recognising the beat. 'It can't be!' groaned Charles. But it was.

Round the corner she came, like a four-footed avenging angel. Downhill now, so there was nothing to hold her up. Wheezing like a bellows with the exertion and shaking Julius roundly at every thud. Leaving her behind and trying to lose her, she snorted when she caught up with us — and, when we tried to placate her, she kicked petulantly out at us and promptly lost her footing in the mud.

We expected Julius to appear at any moment on the way back, but he didn't. Even so we didn't take her up the hill again. She stayed in the Valley now. Receiving her many callers; bulging, so it seemed to me, daily; and beset, as soon as the summer came, by flies.

It so happened that Aunt Louisa had given me some old lace curtains of my grandmother's to put over the raspberries, and when Charles came in one day and said the flies were pestering her badly, couldn't we find something to cover her head and eyes, I said I had the very thing. I got a piece of lace curtain long enough to hang over her nose, cut two holes in it for her ears, put it on and tied it firmly behind her head.

It worked wonders. Admittedly she looked like a Spanish duenna wearing her mantilla back to front — but who, I said, was going to see that, if we kept her grazing quietly on the lawn? The answer was the riding school, who appeared within minutes as if summoned by a bugle. Annabel sauntered over to greet them, putting her head, curtain and all, over the wall; there was a chorus of 'Oooohs' from the children... 'Look Miss Linley, Annabel's getting married' called one excited voice. There was no answer from Miss Linley this time. She was quite at a loss for words.

Before long the flies involved us in a far more serious situation, however. By this time we'd discovered a fly repellent made specially for horses, which we sprayed on her back and legs and — since she objected to the hissing at too close quarters — rubbed by hand round her nose and ears. One warm morning I sprayed her thoroughly as usual, put her to graze on the slope behind the cottage — not far enough to involve her in any real climbing but enough to give her a change of grass — and was coming back down with the fly spray when I suddenly realised that I had the wrong tin. Not the fly repellent for horses but a tin of household fly killer containing Pybuthrin.

I knew what the instructions said without looking at them.

'Remove birdcages and fishbowls ... cover children's cots ... not to be used on cats and dogs...' We never used it at home ourselves. The only reason we had it was that we'd taken it on a trip to the Camargue in the mosquito season — and the only reason it happened to be on hand, which was how I'd picked it up, was that I'd got it out the previous day to give the name of it to Louisa, who was going on her first-ever trip abroad and had visions of deadly insects everywhere from Calais onwards.

When I told Charles what I'd done, his opinion, based on the observation that I'd used it enough on him and he was still around himself, was that it probably wouldn't hurt her at all. She was big, he said. She didn't lick herself as a cat or dog would. Better just watch her for a while, he advised. There was nothing else we could do.

There was, though. After ten minutes of waiting for her to collapse — sure at one moment that she had because I couldn't see her, but it was all right, she was only hidden temporarily behind a tree — I rang up Boots in the nearest town and asked to speak to one of their chemists.

'A what?' was the astonished comment when I told him what I'd done. 'A donkey,' I worriedly confirmed. It was like confiding one's troubles to a policeman. When he said hold on a moment while he consulted his colleagues and incredulous voices saying 'She's sprayed a *what?*' came from the room behind him, the equanimity with which he in turn replied 'A donkey' was really magnificent. There was a muttered conference, after which he returned to the phone to report that the general opinion was that if she were their donkey they'd wash her. 'With what?' I enquired puzzledly. 'Oh, the usual thing — soapflakes or detergent and plenty of hot water,' he said, speaking by now as if it were the most normal thing in the world.

It wasn't, of course. I thanked him, told Charles, and the pair of us started slogging up behind the cottage with buckets of detergent. Better to do the job up there, we decided, where the water could sink into the ground, instead of in the yard where the next thing would be Solomon paddling in it and we'd be ringing up Boots about him.

Which was how — elevated on the hillside as on a stage we were next to be seen industriously bathing a donkey. Rubbing in the detergent till she foamed; running up with buckets of water to rinse her; running up again with the proper fly spray when we'd finished because, having got off all the original repellent, the horse-flies were pitching on her in hundreds as she was now so attractively wet.

'What be doin' up there then?' came Father Adams's voice inevitably, in due course, from the bottom, and when we told him he said we fair beat cock-fighting. When, a few weeks later, he looked over the wall one day and saw me fitting a striped canvas bag with a rubber sole over one of Annabel's feet it was too much even for him, however. 'Don't tell I thee bist making her *boots*?' he declared. And when I confessed that as a matter of fact I was — 'God Almighty!' he breathed incredulously.

There was a logical explanation, of course. There was for most of our actions. It was just the appearance of what we were doing that so often looked peculiar — the snag being that in most cases it is the appearance by which one is judged.

In this case I'd noticed Annabel limping and, thinking maybe one of her hooves needed trimming, I'd called in the farrier. T'wudn't her hooves, he reported after his examination. The little old girl had trodden on a nail. He'd never known it afore with a donkey, he said. Horses, yes — but not donkeys, who usually trod so lightly. There were the hole though, he said, gently squeezing the upturned hoof at which pus came out of it and Annabel whimpered with pain. Us had better get the Vet.

I did. Harler, when he came, expressed no surprise at all on hearing that Annabel was the first donkey the farrier had ever known to get a nail in her foot. He'd never known of one either, he said, but if anybody was going to be first it would undoubtedly be her. Would I mind holding her head?

Actually there was no need. Just as Annabel had stood unmoving for the farrier, so she now stood like a slave in a Roman forum for Mr Harler. He examined her, cleaned her foot and gave her an antibiotic injection in the rump. All we had to do now, he said, ruffling her fringe when he'd finished and telling her that she was a far better patient than a certain Siamese cat he knew, was to soak her foot three times a day in hot water to bring out the pus, and keep it covered to fend off the dirt.

All we had to do indeed. If *he'd* put her foot in a bucket she'd no doubt have stayed there batting her eyelashes at him till the water froze. When we attempted to do it she either took it out again and stuck it determinedly in the dirt, kicked the bucket over, or, if the fancy took her, strolled around the lawn while we strove to move the bucket with her like an outsize Wellington boot.

If we kept her foot in water for a minute we were lucky, and as for covering it afterwards — in the corner of an old nail-bag or something like that, said Mr Harler; heavy canvas so she could walk on it, and tied round her fetlock so she couldn't get it off — we managed that all right. The trouble was, Annabel kept wearing through the canvas.

Whether it was relief at being able to stand on the foot again or a desire to show off about having seen the Vet, she stumped up and down her field so solidly that in two days she went through both corners of the only nail-bag we could get and after that I was reduced to making her foot covers out of a piece of deck-chair canvas. These she went through even more quickly, until I hit on the idea of sewing a rubber heel to the bottom with string — back to front, like a miniature horseshoe, to fit the shape of her foot.

It worked. It was perfectly logical. Even Father Adams had to admit that when it was explained to him. Unfortunately we couldn't explain it to everybody, however, and when Annabel discovered that the rubber heel made a useful digging implement... It wasn't so much that she dug holes all over the lawn with it — what with molehills and drains our lawn was pretty well past praying for in any case. It was the fact that people saw her. In a green and orange-striped boot with a back-to-front rubber heel on it. You can guess what they thought about that. What Miss Wellington wanted to know when she heard we'd had the Vet was what he'd said about Annabel. 'About the *baby*,' she urged insistently. 'Did you ask him if it was *true*?'

As a matter of fact I hadn't. For one thing I didn't think it was fair, having got him along to see to her foot, to ask him to throw in a confirmation that she was in foal — and for another I was perfectly certain she was. The way she bulged, the way she acted — only that very week Janet and I had watched entranced as she stood in the lane, her sides jumping like a Mexican bean with what we were sure was unquestionably Julius.

He would have thought I was nuts, asking him if a donkey bulging so much she looked as if she was wearing panniers under her skin was in foal, I replied to Charles when he in turn, on coming home that night, said but why hadn't I asked Harler to confirm it. All I'd done was *tell* him she was in foal, to make sure the injection wouldn't harm her, and he had said it wouldn't.

It was my fault entirely, therefore, that we still didn't definitely know. July came and went, but no Julius. August came and went, but no Augustus. One night in August I sat with her for ages in her stable, watching her sigh and stamp her feet as she ate and feeling her stomach at cautious intervals for signs of movement. We'd just been told that it took fifty-four weeks — a year and a fortnight — for a donkey to have a foal, as against a horse's eleven months. A year and a fortnight from the time Annabel had been mated would have been that very day and there were signs of movement now all right. Annabel's stomach twitched and she stamped her back feet irritably every time I touched her. Towards midnight, awed by the thought of what the morrow might bring, I went back down to Charles. I wouldn't be a bit surprised if Augustus were here by morning, I told him.

He wasn't. Septimus wasn't there by September, either. We put off our holiday week by week just in case, but by mid-September we'd completely given up hope. We went on holiday and Annabel went to the farm. Not entirely uneventfully. She had her foot in a plaster casing.

Fifteen: Anniehaha

She'd trodden on another nail. He could believe it, said Mr Harler when I rang him once more to tell him. Nothing about our lot would ever surprise *him*. I reckon it would have done if I'd told him how she'd covered everything from eating Yorkshire pudding to side-twitching and still hadn't produced that foal, but I forbore. For his part, either he'd forgotten the foal, decided it was some time in the future — or could it have been, come to think of it, that he knew the story as well as we did and was being professionally tactful? Anyway, neither of us mentioned it.

There was no need for us to postpone our holiday, was all he said. He and his assistants would see that she was all right. So her foot was drained and dressed, swathed in bandage upon bandage like a gout-wrapping, painted with plaster of Paris to keep the bandages dry, and off she went to the farm where Mrs Pursey said anything the little soul wanted, she, too, would willingly do for her. In that case, said Annabel, hopefully pouting her mouth, she'd like some bread-and-butter like Mrs Pursey always gave her, and she got it on the spot.

So there we were again. A perfectly logical explanation about the plaster, but one which was of course quite unknown to the onlookers who saw a small, fat donkey trudging up the hill in what appeared to be a plaster cast, making the most of it as usual and playing the Wounded Donkey Heroine being Taken Into Captivity.

By the time we came back the bandages were off, her foot was completely healed, and our name was mud with the faction who, still under the impression that she was in foal, had decided that she'd had to have the plaster on to support her growing weight, and in that condition… *Poor* little donkey, said one of her sympathisers, at which Annabel snorted in soulful agreement … we'd gone away and heartlessly left her.

Time proved that wrong, as the weeks went by, no foal appeared, and Annabel remained as bulgingly plump as ever. We just couldn't win, though — and neither, so far as that period was concerned, could the Duggans. On one side of them the boat was almost finished, the hammering had long since stopped, everybody was admiring the trim little craft that sat buoyantly in the driveway — and Alan was now worrying in case someone wanted to buy it and the Foots started boat-building all over again. On the other, though the bulldozer was silent at last, the Duggans were now suffering heavily from bonfires as the builder and his helpers cleared the undergrowth.

Not only from the smoke, either. Alan swore that one afternoon he and Carrie were sitting on the lawn — used by now, he said, to being kippered — when an adder four feet long came travelling across it at speed. Definitely an adder, he said, when we queried whether it might not perhaps have been a grass snake. Coming straight for them with its head raised, and by Harry it was touch and go, when he got up and shooed it off, as to whether it jumped at him or not. His theory was that it had been annoyed by the bonfire. It had hissed at him angrily, he said, and then turned tail and slid into the rockery. How many more of the perishing things, he wanted to know, might be there, lying in wait, ready to attack?

None so far as we heard. With the Duggans' star in such temporary eclipse, however, we should have known better than to ask them to look after our garden while we were away. Since everything happened to us, and what didn't happen to us appeared to be happening at the moment to them, it was obviously asking for trouble.

It was, too. We came back to find that Carrie had of all things fallen on our path and dislocated her elbow, and scarcely had we digested that catastrophe — it wasn't our fault, she kept heroically telling us; she hadn't tripped or anything; just one moment she was putting down her basket at the conservatory door and the next she was flat on her face — when I happened to mention Alan and we heard the news about him. He'd nearly poleaxed himself on our plum tree.

It was the very first morning we'd gone, she said. Alan had gone down to open the tomato house, and near the garage he too had fallen down. Why she couldn't imagine, unless it was all that smoke affecting him. Anyway, getting up, irate as anybody would be in the circumstances and with a badly grazed knee, he'd forgotten for the moment where he was and, coming up directly under the plum tree, had caught himself a thumping crack on an overhanging branch and gone down again practically for the count.

Carrie was annoyed with him when he got back. All he'd been asked to do was open the greenhouse door, she said, and he came back limping, mud on his trousers, a cut on his bald head and moss off the plum tree all over him like woad. Just like a man, she'd informed him; she'd much better go herself.

That night she did go herself. Fortunately Alan had taken her down in the car and was sitting in it glowering balefully at the plum tree when she, too, fell down. Nowhere near where he had tripped, she said, and she was standing still and the path was dry and she couldn't for the life of her understand it. He was there, anyway. On hand to run her to the doctor, and then to the nearest hospital, where they'd put her elbow straight under anaesthetic.

She'd never forget it, she said. She'd come round at eleven o'clock at night. There she was with her elbow bandaged and Alan sitting gloomily beside her holding his head... They'd put him to watch her to see that she came round all right and his first heartfelt words, when he saw her open her eyes, were 'And those two so-and-so's are on *holiday*.'

We didn't know whether to laugh or cry. Carrie's accident was awful, and we felt dreadfully sorry about that. But Alan's was so like something out of the *Keystone Cops*... We tried hard to keep our faces straight, and then Carrie started to giggle. If we could have *seen* him, she choked, sitting there in the cubicle with a face as long as a fiddle. 'Bouncing off the plum tree,' I chortled. 'Covered all over with mildew,' roared Charles. 'Lot of unfeeling heathens,' growled Alan.

Meanwhile, having brought Annabel home again, we had to consider her future. To mate or not to mate was the operative question. Normally, if a mating fails, one is entitled to a free re-mating with the original stallion. But Peter had by this time been sold — and even if he hadn't I doubt whether we would have considered it. One thing we'd learned, discussing it in many quarters over recent weeks, was that that particular cross is very difficult. A donkey stallion with a mare, yes. You get mules as easy as winking. A horse with a donkey mare — no. It is something to do with the lack of matching chromosomes. Jennets are rare as roses in April.

There was still no jack donkey around. Even if there had been, said Farmer Pursey, he wouldn't advise us on that. May was the time for mating. We'd be wasting our time in October. So we concentrated on getting Annabel's weight down. Sixty inches she'd measured at the final stretch — round with the tape measure — mostly consisting of Yorkshire Pudding, as we could see it now. Getting so fat had been why she'd baulked at the hill. Keeping her down in the Valley so as not to tire her had made her even fatter. And as for Julius moving ... he'd always had his doubts about that, said Charles; he reckoned it was the flies making her stomach twitch.

It *had* been Julius too, Annabel insisted indignantly. Hurting her foot had put him off. She wouldn't have him at all, mind, she threatened, when we took her for her first reducing walk. As she wasn't having him anyway we took no notice of her objection, got out the bridle we'd bought some months before but had never used because we hadn't wanted, in what we'd thought was her delicate state, to upset her and we put it on.

Farmer Pursey had advised it. A donkey bridle with a little snaffle bit, he'd said. Nothing to hurt her, but we'd control her a lot better on that than with a halter. Let her wear it for a few days for an hour or so on the lawn to get used to it, lead her gently so it didn't pull her mouth — in no time at all we wouldn't know ourselves when we took her out.

After the first couple of times, when we wondered why people were laughing and discovered, when we looked back, that our status symbol was marching along behind us with her mouth wide open, it really worked very well. The bridle had a head-band with red and white triangles on it, and, being Annabel, it was always lopsided so that the effect was that of a slightly tipsy Red Indian squaw, but it suited her. Annabel knew it too, jingling her bit rings with the best of them and regarding the bigger horses, when we met, with the air of being just as good as they were and with a harness like they had, too.

On outward journeys, once she got into the routine again, she still ran loose, gambolling and capering and pretending to kick us as ever. On homeward journeys, however, where in the old days she dallied and dawdled and at times I swear my arm stretched to three times its length trying to get her home, she now walked demurely on her bridle as to the manner born. When I took her to the village she was on her bridle all the time, of course, and it was thus — with Annabel on the lawn one morning harnessed ready for the Post Office and Sheba bawling from the garden wall about brushing her too, she was prettier than silly old donkeys — that I had an idea and put Sheba on her back.

For a moment Sheba looked wildly for the safest way to jump. Then, feeling the warmth coming through to her paws, she settled happily down on Annabel and curled her tail. Why hadn't we thought of this before? she demanded. We knew how her feet got cold.

We led Annabel half a dozen or so steps on her bridle, Sheba squatting happily on her like a little blue-point hen. At that point Annabel, having had enough, buckled her knees to roll and Sheba departed precipitately, but it was a start. After that we often put Sheba on her back and Annabel got used to carrying her for longer and longer distances. The effect would have been quite impressive but for the fact that Sheba didn't mind which way she rode and was more often than not to be seen blissfully proceeding back to front. Even at that it was quite something. We couldn't get Solomon to do it. Only girls liked riding, he informed us, leaping from Annabel's back as though she were a sinking ship the moment we tried to put him on her. Boys preferred eating and fighting.

We had a feeling that Annabel liked Sheba. Perhaps because she was another girl. Perhaps because she was smaller and less boisterous than Solomon. At any rate, Sheba talking to Annabel and Annabel looking down at her with the benevolent big-sister expression on her face with which the larger horses in turn looked down at Annabel was quite a feature of our domestic scene these days. So were the pair of magpies who also struck up a friendship with her and, wherever she was tethered up on the hill, could be depended on to track her down within minutes, pottering companionably about her feet as she grazed, while occasionally — had they spotted Sheba doing it? we wondered — one of them perched on her back and sat there talking quietly to her as she moved about. Only one. Presumably the other one was like Solomon and not in favour of riding. Really there seemed no end to Annabel's friends.

She'd always had plenty of human friends, of course. Miss Wellington, Father Adams, Janet, Mrs Farrell who toasted all the bread she brought with the observation that it was better for Annabel's stomach, and was rewarded by the fact that from her Annabel would take nothing *but* toasted bread. On the odd occasions Mrs Farrell brought a piece untoasted, Annabel snorted and blew it back at her.

There were also the countless mothers and grandmothers who trekked regularly down with small children, pushing prams valiantly through the mud to her gate with offerings of sweets and apples and pacifying the wails of sorrow if our heroine herself were not on view. And later, as they grew up, there were the children themselves, unaccompanied.

There was a trio who came regularly that autumn. Two boys and a girl, all about eight years old. Like angels straight from heaven they looked, though we soon learned to nip out smartly when they were about since they had a most unangelic habit of damming our stream with stones as they passed, so that it flooded straight down the lane.

This presumably was to deter imaginary pursuers, since they then proceeded up on to the hill behind the cottage where, if Annabel was on her tether, she became the centre of a game of Cowboys and Indians. Annabel joined in with a will, following them into ambush under the trees, occasionally knocking somebody's feet from under them with her rope, which was the signal for shrieks of laughter from the children and a complacent snort from Annabel, and looking out as warily as they did when someone passed along the track below.

Alas for our belief that she was probably supposed to be Trigger. They were up there one day with her under a pine tree, pretending to make camp, unloading a couple of make-believe tents from her back… 'Now we'll go and prospect up the hill,' said one of them. 'And mind you keep her hidden from the cowboys,' he instructed the diminutive squaw. 'But aren't we the cowboys?' came a bewildered feminine voice. 'Of course not. We're *Indians*,' was the scornful reply. 'And Anniehaha's our Indian pony.'

All it needed was for them to see Anniehaha going out on her diamond-patterned bridle, of course, and they were on to it at once. Could *they* take her out? they enquired hopefully. Just up the hill and back? 'I go to riding lessons and I know how to handle her,' said the leader of the trio persuasively.

We let her go. She could do with all the exercise she could get to slim down that waistline, we reasoned; and when we first had her children often used to take her out on her halter. It was just a question of her now being on a bridle and the fact that nobody but ourselves had taken her out for more than a year.

We undid her reins, turning them into a single lead-rein so that if she did run she couldn't trip. I trotted beside her myself for part of the way to encourage her to go. Then, instructing them to go no further than the Forestry house and back, I slipped quietly out of the procession and watched them trudging on up the hill. Like a group on a Christmas card, they looked. Two boys — the one holding the lead-rein still informing the others that he knew how to handle her because he went to riding-school — a girl, and a plump little donkey.

It was a far different procession that returned some ten minutes later. In the lead was Annabel, going it like Arkle, with the boy who took riding lessons keeping valiantly up beside her like a Marathon runner. Far behind came the other two, also running, but nowhere in the picture with the leaders.

'Let her go! Let go the rein! We'll field her!' yelled Charles, taking in the situation at once. And field her we did, Annabel snorting with satisfaction as she reached us, while the boy collapsed, completely breathless, on the bank.

He'd run all the way from the Forestry house, he told us when at last he could speak. She'd looked round there, found that I wasn't with her and had decided to come back. He'd *said* he'd look after her, he replied with dignity when we asked but why hadn't he let go of the reins when she started to run. 'You rotters might have helped me though,' he said indignantly to his two companions. The boy muttered sheepishly and kicked at a stone. 'But Roger, you're the one who takes the riding lessons,' said the girl, with wide-eyed innocence.

Sixteen: Like Solomon Only Horse-sized

So there we were. Annabel didn't seem to be doing so badly as a single unit. As if to make up for it, in fact, she seemed more domesticated than ever.

Winter was setting in now. The leaves were off the trees, darkness was falling early, and often, about half-an-hour or so before sunset, we turned her loose in the Forestry lane. We'd proved she wouldn't chew the trees. We knew, from the way she'd come back from the Forestry house, that she wouldn't go far without us. There were rarely any riders about by then and it was good for her, we thought, to wander at random along the hedgerows.

Actually she didn't do much wandering at random. As soon as the lights went on she could be found unfailingly at a point where the Forestry track overlooked a house, built below it into the hillside. There, once it was dusk, stood Annabel. Preserving the proprieties, of course. Pretending to eat most industriously from the hedge. But gawking so intently down through the window at the Pennys' supper preparations that we had practically to carry her home.

Earlier than that she could be found up on the open patch at the top. Grazing along the verge, while she watched Farmer Pursey's cows in the field where I'd done my Cossack dance, and eyeing them between mouthfuls with the superiority of a donkey who, herself, was free to wander.

The best way of getting her back from there was to hammer on her feeding bowl like a dinner gong. Down the hill she'd gallop, line up behind me at the gate and follow as obediently as Mary's lamb while I led her, entirely without halter or bridle, to her stable. True if anyone saw me I felt like the Pied Piper of Hamelin. True there were times when, on account of her being at the far end of the open patch and round the corner, she couldn't hear me banging and I had to trudge up the hill-track hammering lustily as I went. A bit of a nit I felt then, audible to the entire village and as like as not, when she did get wind of it, Annabel so intent on seeing what was in the bowl that we'd then run all the way home, I with the bowl held out so she couldn't get at it, she with her neck outstretched as she tried to reach it, so that anybody who saw us must have thought we were having an egg-and-spoon race.

It was fun when I got her back, though. There are three gates to the cottage. In and out through them all I'd weave in a game of follow-my-leader — Annabel trotting behind me with her ears back in simulated pursuit and, when at last I took her to her paddock, butting me exuberantly on the bottom with her head as I bent to undo the gate-strap and nearly hoisting me over the fence.

The cats were in fine fettle, too. Solomon demonstrated his fitness by tormenting Sheba. Jumping on her, patting her proprietarily on the back legs like a boy bowling a hoop when she didn't move fast enough, and entering rooms not by creeping woefully round the door as he did when he was sick, but robustly, right in the middle with his tail raised. At feeding time he descended the step into the kitchen with the air of the principal boy in pantomime coming down the staircase they have for the finale. 'Enter the Fairy Prince' was undoubtedly Solomon's theme. Sheba played Juliet. In the spare-room wall overlooking our staircase there is a small glassless, rectangular window, put there in the old days to throw light on to the stairs and left there when we had the staircase straightened because we liked its quaintness. Hitherto unreachable, it didn't take Sheba long after the arrival of the piano to discover that she could now stand on the piano-top when closed, look through the window, and frighten the daylights out of anybody who happened to be coming up the staircase with a raucous Siamese wail.

The day Solomon tried, the piano-top was up and, when he landed on it, it shut with such a bang he frightened the daylights out of himself.

That is by the way, however. Sheba now evolved a game whereby every time Charles went upstairs she rushed up ahead of him, jumped on to the piano, put her head through the little window and bawled at him till he answered back. From this she progressed to not merely waiting for Charles to go upstairs but, at least a dozen times a night, standing by the door to the hall and demanding that he should.

So with Sheba being Juliet, Solomon doing pantomime entrances, Annabel happy as a lark spying on other people's suppers ... everybody in fact, just for once, all shipshape and Bristol fashion... Wouldn't you bet that that was when, being us, we took up horse-riding again?

It was coincidence as well, of course. Ever since we went to Scotland there'd been some reason why we couldn't ride. Charles's back; me with a book to write; the cats being ill; Annabel, as we'd thought, in foal and we didn't want to upset her. It just so happened that when Mrs Howell said would we like to ride her Rory, just for once there was nothing to stop us.

She had two horses, Rory and Troy. Troy was her daughter's mount and when Stella was away at school Mrs Howell could be seen harassedly but determinedly exercising him, according to instructions, to keep him in trim for the holidays. Rory was the second horse, purchased as companion for Troy and for riding by Mrs Howell and Stella's friends when Stella herself was at home.

In buying Rory Mrs Howell, envisaging the periods between holidays and half-terms when he would be ridden very little, had stipulated a quiet horse which didn't need much exercise, and that, at the outset, was what she'd got. A thin black horse who'd been overworked and was only too glad, when he was introduced to the lush green pastures of the Moat House, to stay there, eating his fill of the clover, trailing his long black legs in the dew, and presumably talking to Troy — which was what he was there for — when Troy came back from riding and wanted company.

Time had wrought startling changes, however. A few months of rest and good feeding and Rory now looked what he was. A young, slender-legged part-Arab raring to go. Complimentary as this was to the Howells, it now meant that the sight of Mrs Howell frantically exercising Troy in between her other activities was often followed, an hour or two later, by the sight of her frantically exercising Rory as well. If we could ride him sometimes, she said, reining him breathlessly at our gate one day, it would help her out considerably.

Would we ride him? We jumped at the chance! Beautiful, black, long-legged — like Solomon only horse-sized, the thought flashed through my mind… Any time she liked, we assured her enthusiastically.

Like Solomon only horse-sized was right. Charles rode him like a centaur, but the first time I took him out alone we got no further than the Rose and Crown when he said he was going home.

It was his affection for Troy that did it. That was actually why I was out with him alone. With Troy he got all boisterous and tried to run races; he was better behaved on his own. So long, that was, as you didn't let him look behind and realise that Troy wasn't with him, which I'd unfortunately done and which was why we were now going in circles, he determined to go back and be with his friend while I, equally determined, strove to get him round the corner.

One must never let a horse have his way, of course, or from then on he'll be the master. I'd hardly say I had my way either since eventually I had to get off and ignominiously walk him round, but it was the best I could do in the circumstances. It was opening time. The regulars were beginning to arrive for their midday pints. Round the corner, I thought, I could remount in quiet seclusion.

Like heck I could. Round the corner I met Alan Duggan and Father Adams. 'Want any help?' called Alan gleefully. 'Hurt theeself?' hopefully roared Father Adams.

Aware that the consensus of opinion in the pub, once those two got there, would undoubtedly be that I'd fallen off, I walked dignifiedly on down the lane, selected a quiet spot and attempted to re-mount. At the Moat House I'd done it with a mounting-block. The snag out here in the lane was that I couldn't get my foot up to the blasted stirrup.

Always resourceful, I led Rory to the nearby bank, stood on it and attempted to get on from there. Rory, spotting a clump of grass at the top that he fancied, promptly mounted the bank with his forefeet himself, I couldn't get on him at that angle and, hearing footsteps coming up the hill, I hastily hauled him down and we nonchalantly resumed our stroll just as Fred Ferry hove to around the corner.

'Nice day,' said Fred. It certainly was, I said. A little later I tried again.

Right, in my desperation, outside Miss Wellington's where I stood in the middle of the road, at last got my foot into the stirrup, hoisted myself with a tremendous heave and came down, undoubtedly to her complete stupefaction, not in Rory's saddle, but behind it.

As if that was my normal way of mounting I slipped unruffledly into the saddle, resumed my stirrups, prepared to trot along… It was no use. Rory said he didn't mind my walking with him but if I rode him he was going home to Troy, we started going in giddy circles in the road, and off I got once more…

Many a ride I had on him after that, and he became Charles's favourite horse. That, however, is another story. That first time I took him out is engraved like Calais on my heart.

Even when I'd walked him down to the Valley it wasn't the end of it. Annabel, aghast at my bringing home a *horse*, stood and ho-hooed her disapproval on the hillside, the cats appeared on the garden wall like grandstand spectators at Ascot, Charles said I must get on and ride him *immediately* or I'd never have control of him again.

I did. Charles led him part-way to get him going. The cats craned their necks at us. Annabel bawled. At the top of the hill, pinning her hat on hurriedly as she came, appeared Miss Wellington, hastening to see what was happening…

Nobody misses anything in our village.

A NOTE TO THE READER

If you have enjoyed Doreen Tovey's Memoir enough to leave a review on **Amazon** and **Goodreads**, then we would be truly grateful.

Sapere Books is an exciting new publisher of brilliant fiction and popular history.

To find out more about our latest releases and our monthly bargain books visit our website: **saperebooks.com**

62794047R00086

Made in the USA
Columbia, SC
05 July 2019